Black Time

D1595408

BLACK TIME

Fiction of Africa, the Caribbean,
and the United States

BONNIE J. BARTHOLD

New Haven and London

Yale University Press

Published with assistance from the foundation established in memory of
Henry Weldon Barnes of the Class of 1882, Yale College.

Designed by Nancy Ovedovitz and set in Baskerville type.
Printed in the United States of America by Vail-Ballou Press,
Binghamton, N.Y.

Library of Congress Cataloging in Publication Data

Barthold, Bonnie J.   1940-
   Black time.

   Bibliography: p.
   Includes index.
   1. Fiction—Black authors—History and criticism. 2. African fiction
(English)—Black authors—History and criticism. 3. Caribbean fiction
(English)—Black authors—History and criticism. 4. American fiction—
Afro-American authors—History and criticism. 5. Time in literature. I. Title.
PN841.B3   809.3′938   80-24336
ISBN 0-300-02573-4

10   9   8   7   6   5   4   3   2   1

To my mother

Contents

Preface

During the past century, and especially the past twenty-five years, black writers have published scores of novels that in one way or another embody the black experience. Increasingly during the past decade or so, writers from Africa and the Caribbean, as well as the United States, have added their vision to this body of literature. This book is based upon the premise that this fiction is both unified enough and singular enough to justify its study as a separate aspect of modern literature as well as an important feature of contemporary culture. This does not mean that black fiction—or black culture—exists in a hermetically sealed compartment cut off from the larger world, or that it is inherently better or worse than other fiction or culture. But, broadly speaking, fiction springs from experience, and a black heritage differs in some crucial ways from a Western European heritage. The book has been divided into four parts in order to approach the subject comprehensively.

The first part undertakes to provide the necessary historical background, focusing specifically on the black experience of time. Part 2 considers certain characteristic themes and forms in black fiction, relating them to the writers' manipulation of time. In the third part, seven representative novels are discussed. The epilogue considers briefly certain theoretical ramifications of the book's focus on time.

In a somewhat different form, much of the material on the African novelists appeared in my 1975 doctoral dissertation for the University of Arizona: "Three West African Novelists: Chinua Achebe, Wole Soyinka, and Ayi Kwei Armah." In that effort, the encouragement and stimulation of my dissertation committee were indispensable. I extend my gratitude to Richard Smyer, Oliver Sigworth, Sidonie Smith, Fred Rebsamen, and Ingeborg Kohn.

Again with regard to the African portion of the discussion, I am indebted to Kwadwo Oduro for his assistance with the Akan translations and to Victor Esan for help with the Yoruba.

The book in its present form was begun with the help of a summer grant from the National Endowment for the Humanities in 1977. The chapter on women has been strengthened by my participation in "Women in American Literature," a seminar sponsored during the summer of 1979 by the National Endowment under the direction of Martha Banta of the University of Washington. Her insights generally have proven invaluable.

Without the encouragement of Asa Davis of Amherst College, this book might never have been begun.

I am grateful to my colleagues at Adams State College—Joan Foster, especially—for their support and encouragement.

Above all, I thank my daughter, Amma, for not only bearing with me but cheering me on.

PART 1
THE HISTORICAL
BACKGROUND

Black Time:
The Reality
versus
the Myth

The novelist, by making time do his bidding, metaphorically *can* "make his sun stand still" and "make him run," too. For the novel, unlike drama, there are no received conventions restraining the use of time. The novelist has from the beginning had absolute freedom in his approach to time. And before there were novels there were tales, the progenitor of the prose narrative, the teller of which could cover decades, centuries, or minutes as he chose. The teller of tales, no less than the contemporary novelist, was above all the puppet master of time; and in some sense it must be recognized that the essence of the prose narrative, novel as well as tale, lies in its manipulation of time, with the implication that the teller or the writer has thereby achieved a symbolic victory over his own mortality.

In the prefaces of *Tom Jones*, Fielding notes that some scenes are best rendered in full, some dealt with summarily, and others skipped over entirely, and that the choice is a matter of the writer's judgment. Some of the most memorable novels or scenes within novels are memorable because of what happens to time. *The Sound and the Fury*, *Tristram Shandy*, *Bleak House*, *To the Lighthouse*—in each a radical conception and presentation of time structures the narrative. The trip to the poorhouse scene in Conrad's *The Secret Agent* is memorable because of its dilation of time, a slowing down reminiscent in many ways of certain scenes in Dickens's novels. Throughout *Under the Volcano*, Malcolm Lowry telescopes time, achieving a sense that present unfolding is simultaneous with past occurrence. The science fiction writer has available the convention of time travel, and uses it to explore, for example, the boundaries between determinism and free will. In Joyce Carol Oates's *Them*, part of the maddeningly effective structure is an ironic pace: murders are over in the blink of an eye as women sit interminably around tables.

Like all fiction writers, the black novelist plays a game shaped by his experience with mortality, alternately reflecting or rebelling against his knowledge that he is, ultimately, time's fool. But his victimization by time has historically taken a somewhat different shape from the victimization experienced by the peoples of Western European cultures, and because of this his fiction, too, is different. To understand these differences in black fiction, it is necessary to chart them as they have occurred in history, beginning at the point where black history begins, on the continent and in the culture of Africa. This summary is perhaps doubly important because of the distortions and omissions that have, until recently, characterized the writing of black history.

Africa has, in fact, typically generated more symbols than it has history. From the time of Othello, it has been associated with flamboyance, mystery, power, and destruction. Since Rousseau, it has often been linked with notions of noble savagery. Graham Greene sees it as the focus of a Victorian death wish, embodied, for example, in Rider Haggard's *She*.[1] For Joseph Conrad's Kurtz and Saul Bellow's Henderson, Africa is where a person's past is lost and where the true self emerges. In the Tarzan books and others of their ilk, the symbol lapses into the cliché of mysteriousness that lends the impossible an air of credibility. Nègritude writers, selecting from these symbols, chose to see Africa as the milieu of spiritual regeneration for a machine-subjugated world. In Frantz Fanon's *The Wretched of the Earth*, a portion of Africa becomes symbolic of the destructive oppres-

---

1. Cited by Per Wästberg, "Introduction," *The Writer in Modern Africa*, p. ix.

sion worked by the peoples of the West on those of the Third World. Long after its rivers and its mountains have been charted, "Africa" is as much a concept—many, often contradictory, concepts—as it is a continent.

In the daily newspaper one encounters Africa in images of drought, coups, wars, and starvation. Rarely is one encouraged to see Africa in terms of the quotidian—of family quarrels, personal disappointments, domestic virtues, quiet love, or any of the other homely parts that comprise a large share of human experience. Africa, as Joyce Cary has noted, demands the dramatic and the flamboyant. As a symbol, Africa alternates between the savage and the idyllic. At its most complex, it fuses the two into a kind of savage splendor.

The symbol is clearly not the reality, and nowhere is this more true than in the symbolism with which time in Africa has often been endowed. In Western thought, time and Africa are often mutually exclusive. There is the colonial official in countless films who reminds us that "Africans don't know the meaning of time." In European and American novels, Africa is a place of lost cities, lost races, and lost time. Kurtz loses his past and his soul; Henderson loses his past and finds his soul. In real life, W. E. B. DuBois goes to Ghana and loses his past but gains his heritage. In the language of the press, Africa is "developing," and part of what is developing is time: Africa is "catching up" with the times, and with time. In its more malevolent, South African aspect, the Bantustan is a place where the "native" can develop "at his own rate," and thus the apartness of apartheid devolves on the assumption that African time is different from the time of the Afrikaner.

To help sift the real from the symbolic, a recent remark by John Updike is illuminating: "A village-born mission-taught, Oxford-anointed African has lived a synopsis of human history. He has outgrown pre-history so quickly that nothing has had time to die; the village gods, the Christian God and the modern absence of God coexist in him."[2] Updike suggests that for the contemporary educated African, time has accelerated radically.

2. John Updike, "Books: Shades of Black," p. 83.

The picture drawn is one in which the concept of "future shock" described by Alvin Toffler (largely in reference to highly technological societies) is multiplied geometrically, as though Western history from pre-Renaissance times to the Apollo moonshots were telescoped into the lifetime of a single person. Though it is true, as Richard Wright has remarked, that "to a greater or less degree, almost all human life on earth today can be described as moving away from traditional, agrarian, simple handicraft ways of living toward modern industrialization,"[3] this movement in twentieth-century Africa (as in other developing areas of the world) has taken place with a startling velocity.

Moreover, the beginning and end points of the movement Wright describes imply very different concepts of time itself: not only does time accelerate in this movement, it also changes its configuration. An agrarian culture, as Lévi-Strauss suggests, conceptualizes time as predominantly synchronic whereas in an industrialized society a diachronic view of time predominates. Summarizing the differences between the two concepts of time, Maxwell writes: "All men experience both change and periodicity, and they may emphasize either change, which lends culture a historical orientation, or periodicity, leading to systems of classification. . . . Whole cultures can be characterized by their preference for one over the other."[4] Thus, the movement Wright describes implies a movement from an emphasis on synchrony, from what other writers have termed "mythic" or "cyclic" time, toward diachrony, toward a preference for history in which time is seen as a linear sequence.

With reference to time, the cultural shift described by Wright is shown graphically in figure 1.

The first stage represents the configuration of time in a traditional, agrarian culture—for example, pre-European Africa and, in the following discussion, specifically the culture of the Guinea Coast. The third stage represents the linearity time has assumed in a highly industrialized culture like that of the United States. In between is the interval of passage, the simultaneous

3. Richard Wright, Introduction to George Lamming, *In the Castle of My Skin*, p. v.
4. Robert J. Maxwell, "Anthropological Perspectives," p. 52.

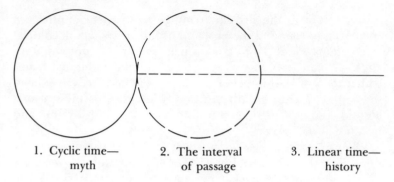

1. Cyclic time—   2. The interval   3. Linear time—
   myth   of passage   history

Figure 1

erosion of the cycle and the development of linearity. The shift described by Wright corresponds with a movement from synchrony to diachrony in time, from a conceptualization of time that rejects change to one that is able to embrace change and thus potentially at least to lend it order. In fact, however, the diagram as given belies the potential complexity of a historic conceptualization of time, which includes "the interplay of a number of durations . . . a recognition of the 'multiplicity of time.' "[5] Instead of the unity of the cycle, a unity dependent upon the rejection of change, in Guillen's view what one has is a linear simultaneity, a diversity of linear "currents" that, taken together, characterize time during a given moment or period. In this view, diachrony assumes a far greater complexity than the diagram indicates; and the synopsis of time suggested by Updike is, accordingly, even more intricate than the diagram implies.

Interestingly, in his most recent statement concerning Africa, embodied in *The Coup*, Updike offers a rendering of this temporal synopsis. Set in an imaginary (Chad-like) country of Kush, the novel offers, instead of "lost time" or "timelessness," temporal chaos: American Hit Parade songs of the fifties ("Cry Me a River," "Que Sera, Sera") coincide with a science-fiction-like portrayal of technology; the main character is a Muslim who does not believe in God, a ruler who has no faith in government,

5. Claudio Guillen, "Second Thoughts," p. 440.

a deserter from the French Army between Dienbienphu and the Algerian war, and the husband of four wives whose cultural orientations range from traditional fatalism to contemporary angst—a man who, in sum, combines certain traditional forms with a 1978 state of unbelief. At the novel's end, he is in exile in the south of France with the only wife who fits his spiritual identity—an eclectic dilettante who cherishes both Braque and traditional African art.

What exists in present-day Africa is a state of temporal flux not unlike that portrayed in *The Coup*, a flux with far-reaching implications for the black experience, not only in Africa but in the New World as well. In fact, the uncertain contingencies of time, as will be shown, lie at the center of black history.

Beginnings: The West African Cycle

In pre-European Africa, the Guinea Coast was a unified cultural area extending south and east from Port Guinea to present-day Cameroon in a strip two to three hundred miles wide. Today, what remains of this traditional culture plays a part in the reality of present-day Guinea, Ivory Coast, Sierra Leone, Gambia, Ghana, Togo, Benin, Nigeria, and Cameroon. A very small part of the African continent, it is nevertheless the area from which most New World slaves were brought and (as part of the attempt to lend greater credibility to the relationships drawn between African and New World writers) the area from which all the African novelists discussed in parts 2 and 3 hail. Thus, the Guinea Coast is the place of origin, by implication if not in fact, of all writers who are later discussed, both those from Africa and those from the New World. In sum, the Guinea Coast can be presumed as the cultural birthplace of black fiction.

There is little doubt that a mythic concept of time was part of Guinea Coast traditional culture and that the same was true of traditional Africa generally. Willie Abraham points out that the "temporal and the non-temporal" were not "unbridgeable" in the African world view, and suggests that this continuity comes out of a cyclic conceptualization of time. Janheinz Jahn remarks that "Africa is only now emerging from the age of myth . . . into the mainstream of history." J. S. Mbiti asserts that "the linear concept of time, with an indefinite past, present and infinite future is practically foreign to African thinking." And according to Mircea Eliade, the culture of traditional tribal groups of this area was characterized by religious beliefs that included the cyclic regeneration of time and the abolition of history.[6]

The conceptualization of time shapes, and is shaped by, a way of life. In pre-European Africa the view of time as cyclic was inextricable from beliefs and practices regarding birth, marriage, and death; it provided in its emphasis on human responsibility the basis for an optimistic religion; and it shaped a philosophy of political leadership founded on community responsibility. Metaphysically, *being* was equivalent to *duration*: each moment embodied a recurrence of a past moment, and implied was a potential future recurrence, so long as the cycle remained unbroken. Time included, or perhaps "belonged to," the community as a whole; "timelessness" was a dread concept, representing estrangement from both the community and the duration implicit in cyclic continuity.

Cyclic recurrence could bear the notion of fatality in which, for example, a series of stillbirths or early deaths of a woman's children was seen not as a serial sequence but as the recurrent embodiment of the same malicious spirit, known in various Guinea Coast vernaculars as *abiku, ogbanje, dzikwidzikwi,* or *awomawu,* all of which literally translate as "born-die." Both the "natural and good" and the "natural and evil" were seen as cyclic.

Moreover, the cycle could broken. When Okonkwo, in Nigerian writer Chinua Achebe's *Things Fall Apart* (set largely in traditional Ibo culture), breaks the Week of Peace that precedes the planting of crops, the community sees his act as jeopardizing the cyclic continuity of the seasons. Okonkwo has offended the goddess of the earth and potentially disrupted natural process. The community has the responsibility to nurture, both maintain

6. Willie Abraham, *The Mind of Africa*, p. 52; Janheinz Jahn, *Muntu: An Outline of the New African Culture*, pp. 12–13; J. S. Mbiti, *African Religions and Philosophy*, p. 22: Mircea Eliade, Foreword, *The Myth of the Eternal Return*, pp. 52–53.

and restore, the temporal continuum. Implied in this responsibility is an ideology which, as Basil Davidson points out,

> may reasonably be called optimistic, for generally [it] taught the supremacy of man in controlling or influencing his own present or future. Far from imposing a grim subjection to the "blind forces" of nature, it held to a shrewd realism. *Onipa ne asem* say the Akan: it is mankind that matters—meaning, in this context, that any man can always be responsible for himself.[7]

In this view, crop failure implied a human failure—a successful harvest implied that the community had succeeded in controlling the cycle of the seasons to its own advantage.

The community also had the responsibility of demonstrating reverence for those who had lived before. This has been termed "ancestor worship," but the phrase is only loosely applicable. Ancestral spirits were the intermediaries between the material world and the spiritual world who "provided the means of protecting the present, guaranteeing the future and generally assuaging doubts and worries."[8] They were spirit guardians, but again their efficacy depended on human fulfillment of responsibility. They could weaken from neglect or lack of reverence, and evil would then find it easier to intrude into the present. If the "peace with the fathers" was not kept, the result could be personal or societal catastrophe. A disruption of the continuity between the living and the dead was tantamount to spiritual chaos, which could manifest itself, for example, in crop failure, impotency, barrenness, or untimely death.

Within the tenets of this belief, birth implied a passage from the spirit world to the material world. Death—a different kind of birth—implied a passage from the material world back to the spirit world. Accordingly, the cyclic continuity between the two worlds was perhaps most vulnerable where issues of birth and death were involved. Children were necessary to maintain the continuity of the cycle, and childlessness was viewed as the "worst fate" that could befall an African.[9] Marriage was seen as

---

7. Basil Davidson, *The African Genius*, pp. 146–47.
8. Ibid., p. 49.
9. Jahn, p. 109.

inextricable from procreation and therefore sacred. Thus, the rituals surrounding childbirth, marriage, and death as well were essentially invocations to spirit guardians to maintain the cycle. If these rituals were not fulfilled, the result could be disaster. In *Things Fall Apart*, Ezeudu notes the consequences of improper burial: "They [members of a neighboring village] throw away large numbers of men and women without burial. And what is the result? Their clan is full of the evil spirits of these unburied dead, hungry to do harm to the living" (p. 33). The passage between the spirit world and the material world was at best risky, and if the rituals of birth and death were left unfulfilled, the cycle could be broken, leaving the spirits of the dead or the unborn to wander, angry with the human community whose ritual negligence had excluded them from the spiritual continuum of the living and the dead.

Sacrifice emphasized the human "manipulation" of the spirit world and was a means of ensuring harmony between the human community and that world.[10] Thus, at the end of *Things Fall Apart*, we leave the village elders about to offer sacrifices to cleanse the land after Okonkwo's suicide. The sacrificial object could be liquor used in the pouring of a libation; a portion of the harvest set aside for the god; a chicken, a ram, or even a human being. The notion of sacrifice postulates a greed on the part of the deity or spirits being propitiated, and understandably greed increased in proportion to the seriousness of the offense or the importance of harmony to a specific human endeavor, e.g., the harvest. In sum, it was by means of sacrifice that the cyclic continuity was preserved or renewed.

Politically, the leader—the chief or king—was also a spiritual leader. Concomitantly, the power of the priest was in part political. The inseparability of spiritual and political leadership is emphasized by Basil Davidson, who points out: "The original nature of kings is to be sought in ritual specialism associated with the guardianship of ancestral charters. . . . They were political and therefore earthly persons as well as ritual and therefore spiritual ones. The two sorts of quality hung inherently to-

10. Davidson, p. 191.

gether. . . . But the spiritual quality remained always paramount.[11] This interrelationship is exemplified in the nature of the power held in Achebe's *Arrow of God* by an Ibo priest, who is described as "half spirit" and "half human" and in his ritual appearances carries in his right hand "nne Ofo, the mother of all staffs of authority in Umuaro" (p. 80). The priest-chief functioned as the "shepherd" of time, not its owner, but on behalf of the community, its keeper, his responsibility to maintain the cyclic continuum simultaneously both a spiritual and political obligation.

11. Ibid., p. 191.

The Linear New World and the Balancing Act

In some sense, mythic time is the sacred time of religion generally, in which ritual re-creates the archetype, say, of the Last Supper. But the extent to which mythic time characterizes a culture depends on the relative strength of the religious versus the secular. In the West, the growing dominance of scientific thought and technology since the Renaissance has coincided with an increasing secularization of culture, recognition of which is a commonplace of modern thought. Today, in a highly industrialized country such as the United States, time is clearly linear rather than cyclic—in the languages of the West, it is "long" or "short," one may be "ahead of time" or "behind time" or "out of time." The emphasis is on progress and change rather than on recurrence. And progress is a linear, forward movement—in Marxist thought a dialectical progression, in capitalism a socioeconomic evolution along the lines of social Darwinism. Though capitalism, unlike Marxism, has sought a reconciliation with religion, it is an uneasy peace that rests equally on intellectual dishonesty and on the erosion of sacred time. In sacred time, God is immanent or manifest in each recurring moment; as time becomes linear and discontinuous, God becomes transcendent. A being whose wholeness disallows fragmentation, He moves beyond time to the transcendent timelessness of eternity. Timelessness in the Western sense thus signifies, in direct opposition to traditional Africa, sacred time; and, again in radical opposition to traditional Africa, sacred time is divorced from human time. Religious ritual becomes a window on timelessness, a way of effacing momentarily the linear fragmentation of the humanly profane.

Human time becomes individual and solitary rather than communal in scope. The human relationship to time typically becomes one of individual ownership, a relationship reflected in idioms that show that, as the saying goes, time is money: the object of private ownership, it can be spent, wasted, lost, found, taken, or stolen like so many golden doubloons. He who owns money owns time and therefore power; and the prisoner who "does time," who "puts in his time," thus "pays his debt to society." Idiomatically, time can be used to show contempt, as in "I wouldn't give him the time of day." But the willing listener or the eager car salesman, perhaps gesturing with outspread arms, indicates that "his" time is "your" time: though he owns it, you are welcome to share it.

This concept of individual ownership, rooted in the secular, becomes the mode of sacred time as well. Calvinistic determinism, for example, singles out the individual for salvation, which is the ultimate transcendence of time. The "inner light" of the Society of Friends posits a direct relationship between the individual and God's timelessness. Both sacred and human time become individual rather than communal in scope. In sacred terms, if the individual ownership of time is denied, one is damned; but the spiritual metaphor is rooted in the reality of human affairs.

Those who are economically dispossessed are often dispossessed of time as well, as anyone who has waited in an urban public health clinic knows. A specifically racial example of the ownership of time is represented in the 1954 U.S. Supreme Court decision, in *Brown* v. *Board of Education*, which said that racial integration was to occur "with all deliberate speed." What constituted "deliberate" and what constituted "speed" was left up to the predominantly white local schoolboard owners of time.

The owners of time may manipulate time to their own advantage. In the post-Reconstruction American South this power was demonstrated in the "grandfather clause," which gave unconditional voting rights only to citizens whose grandfathers had been eligible to vote, denying the black vote by denying the black possession of time.

In a conversation with Margaret Mead, James Baldwin has described his sense of temporal dispossession: "The past is the present. . . . I am one of the dispossessed. According to the West I have no history [yet] my life was defined by the time I was five by the history written on my brow."[12] Black people have experienced time differently from white people, Baldwin argues, because they have been simultaneously deprived of time and fixed in it by the color of their skin. What he says implies the lack of both a past and a freely determined future. Insofar as the West is successful in imposing this view, the black man is both cut off from his African past and denied participation in the Western future. He is stuck in an eternal now over which he has no control, cut off and dispossessed from both the mythic cycle of Africa and the linear flow of Western time.

The linear time of contemporary Western cultures contrasts radically with the cyclic continuum. Sacred time has been divorced from human time. "Timelessness" has come to imply an experience of sacred time rather than an estrangement from cyclic continuity. The individual ownership of time has replaced the sense that the wholeness of time is inextricable from the wholeness of the community. In short, time has become fragmented; and one consequence has been that large numbers of people have been dispossessed of time. Because of economic dispossession and the color of their skin, black people in particular have been segregated not only from the larger community but from time as well, as contemporary Western culture has constructed a barrier at the far end of the interval of passage between cyclic and linear time. For large numbers of black people in the New World, the diagram given earlier needs to be amended as shown in figure 2. The barrier excludes blacks from realizing the ownership of time, while simultaneously compelling them to suffer the consequences of this concept of

12. James Baldwin and Margaret Mead, *A Rap on Race*, pp. 193, 228, 205.

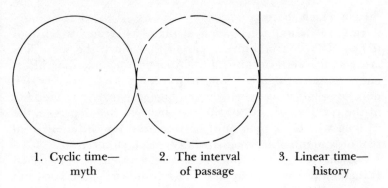

1. Cyclic time—   2. The interval   3. Linear time—
   myth   of passage   history

Figure 2

time. Symbolically, too, there is another barrier that cuts them off from the cyclic continuum of traditional Africa, which can be shown in figure 3. While denying blacks access to progress and the future, Western culture has simultaneously and systematically sought to deny the black past. Until recently the Western concept was that black history was a void, that time began for blacks at the moment when they encountered Western civilization.

One contingency, then, that has shaped black life in the New World down to the present day has been the possibility of temporal dispossession, a life lived predominantly in this interval of

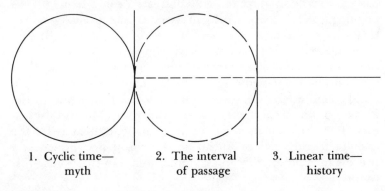

1. Cyclic time—   2. The interval   3. Linear time—
   myth   of passage   history

Figure 3

flux in which there is no past, no future. If in contemporary Africa the radical acceleration of time has created a sense of temporal flux, it becomes apparent that much the same flux arose on the western shore of the Atlantic, for somewhat different reasons. In the twentieth century, being black may very well imply dwelling in a perpetually contingent state of time. Because of the relative strength of this possibility for black people, the dynamics of black time must be recognized as different from that of contemporary mainstream Western culture.

Possibility, however, is not necessarily equivalent to actuality. It is an index to the strength of black people in both Africa and the New World that various forms of rebellion against this attempted victimization have arisen. From one point of view, the history of black people during the past millennium has been the history of a people's rebellion against the uncertainties of time, a balancing act of circumstance and heritage that, viewed closely, assumes heroic proportions, both in Africa and in the New World.

The Guinea Coast has been in contact with Europe since the tenth century; intermittently first, when overland trade routes cut southward from the Sahara and intersected the medieval kingdoms of Songhai and Ghana. This early contact was primarily with Muslim culture, but indirectly the trade routes connected the Guinea Coast with Europe. In the fifteenth century, Portuguese explorers established forts along the Guinea Coast, bases for trade in guns and gold and later, coincident with the opening up of the New World, in slaves. By the seventeenth century, the Portuguese had been joined by the Dutch, British, French, Swedes, and Danes. The traders were followed by missionaries, who introduced Christianity and to some extent Western education and medicine. By the late nineteenth century, political colonization by Europe (punctuated, if not begun, by the Berlin Conference in 1884) was well under way. Much of the history of Africa in the twentieth century can be summarized as the attempt to rid itself of European control, if not influence, a process that predictably will continue well into the twenty-first century.

Until quite recently, African resistance to this European onslaught has been underestimated as the notion has been perpetuated that "historically, Africa's mood in face of Europe has indeed been passive."[13] In actuality, African resistance was continuous, all-pervasive, and multifaceted. Early warfare and "antiwitchcraft" campaigns sought the aid of traditional religion in ridding the land of the European embodiment of evil. Later, direct resistance took the form of nationalistically oriented economic boycotts and political agitation for self-rule, some of which erupted into violence. Both early and late, as Basil Davidson has shown, indirect resistance came from the inherent strength of a highly structured social order that had been evolving for centuries before the advent of the Europeans. Only in the past thirty or forty years has the extent of the complexity of pre-European Africa become known to the West. And contrary to popular misconception,

what emerges is the picture of a complex and subtle process of growth and change behind and within the technological simplicities of former times. The societies still partially observable . . . were and are the terminal structures of an ancient evolution. . . . [African] technological simplicity was no guide to their social and cultural achievement. In truth they had tamed a continent.[14]

African resistance to Europe has fostered the retention of a traditional cultural heritage: "Everywhere the traditional culture meaningfully survives."[15] As anthropologist Melville Herskovits points out, for example, traditional African religions are still a part of contemporary African life and

continue to manifest vitality everywhere. This is to be seen in the worship of African deities, the homage to the ancestors, and the recourse to divination, magic and other rituals. A growing number of Africans, to be sure, have been taught to regard the religion of their forefathers as superstition and to reject other beliefs and customs as outmoded. But

13. Adrian Roscoe, *Mother Is Gold*, p. 2.
14. Davidson, p. 252.
15. Leonard Doob, "The Psychological Pressure upon Modern Africans," p. 376.

there is no evidence which supports the assumption that so often underlies thinking about Africa's future, that African culture, whether in its religious or other aspects, will shortly and inevitably disappear.[16]

Another—and contradictory—misconception about Africa continues to be held: the stereotype of an "uncivilized" Africa filled with wild animals and noble savages, unchanged since time immemorial—the "timeless" Africa of the paradigms of Western thought. This viewpoint underestimates not only the complexity of traditional African culture but also the impact of the West. Actually, the tenacity of African culture coexists with a strong Western influence, and as Herskovits says, "there is no African culture which has not been affected in some way by European contact."[17]

The balance that has been achieved between traditional African culture and Western influence reflects an essential facet of African culture: its well-documented capacity to absorb foreign influence into existing institutions. There is no single explanation for this ability, which in fact preceded Western influence in Africa. African people had periods of great migrations caused, for example, by population pressures, by the need for new and more fertile farmland, or by the encroachment of hostile neighbors. In the course of these migrations, old gods and old customs were retained but out of respect or expediency those of the new area were also adopted. Thus, the Yoruba people of Nigeria have two names to designate the supreme deity, one of them the premigration name used in their former homeland and the other an adaptation of the word then in use among the peoples in the area to which they migrated.[18]

The effects of this balancing act can be seen everywhere in contemporary West Africa. The well-to-do African may pour a traditional libation invoking the blessing of ancestral spirits, and use Johnny Walker in place of, say, *akpeteshie*, a local gin. He may eat palm nut soup from imported china and use sterling

16. Melville Herskovits and William R. Bascom, "The Problem of Stability and Change in African Culture," p. 3.

17. Ibid.

18. Davidson, pp. 51–52.

silver instead of his hand. The African woman may have her baby in a modern maternity hospital and carry it home on her back. Traditional musical instruments are used to play popular songs, and the samba and rumba rhythms that grew out of the West African traditional music exported to South America by means of the slave trade have been reborrowed in West African "highlife" music.[19] The Onitsha market pamphlets, West African best-sellers, present a curious mixture of the didactic African proverb spiced with American slang, with morally couched examples to show the evils of illicit sexual behavior, sometimes with a cover showing models from Spiegel's catalog.[20] Traditional oral literature, too, has adapted and fused various cultural strands with "a story being orally narrated about, say, struggling for political office or winning the football pools. . . . University lecturers can seek to further their own careers and standing by hiring praise singers and drummers to attend the parties given for their colleagues and to panegyricize orally the virtues of hosts and guests."[21]

Perhaps the most striking accommodation may occur in religious belief—the balancing act of certain traditional Fanti priests, for example, as described in the late fifties by James Christensen:

Becoming a Christian while still retaining traditional beliefs need not conflict for the African, for adoption of a new deity does not necessarily imply negation of the old; it is rather to be regarded as an additive factor for protection against the uncertainties of life. All of the priests [of the traditional Fanti priesthood] stated that they had Christians among their clients. The tenacity of the indigenous religion is illustrated by the fact that several priests stated that they had been practicing Christians before their apprenticeships, and one priestess reported that her initial possession by her god occurred while she was attending a Methodist service.[22]

19. Alan P. Merriam, "African Music," in Herskovits and Bascom, p. 82.
20. Emmanuel Obiechina, *An African Popular Literature*, passim.
21. Ruth Finnegan, *Oral Literature in Africa*, pp. 33–34.
22. James Christensen, "The Adaptive Functions of the Fanti Priesthood," in Herskovits and Bascom, p. 270.

Christianity in West Africa may include such elements of traditional African religion as possession by a traditional deity. This inclusion was perhaps encouraged—unwittingly, to be sure—by early translators of the Bible, who often translated the word *God* into African vernaculars. Thus, in Akan-speaking areas of Ghana, Christian hymns are sung to "Onyame." Moreover, new cults may spring up that are neither traditionally African nor yet essentially Christian. The Tigari cult in Ghana, for example, fuses elements of Christianity, Islam, and traditional African religions from an alien area of Upper Volta.[23]

In innumerable ways, then, Guinea Coast culture has proven resilient. This resilience has allowed the accommodation, without the domination, of European culture, as the new has not negated the old. Implied in this resilience is the retention of a traditional cyclic concept of time alongside the linear fragmentation introduced by Europe: as facets of traditional culture have remained intact, so probably has the concept of time. The retention of the African past, including the concept of time as mythic, has proven effective against European domination. Seen in this light, the retention and celebration of the traditional cycle have, as they did in traditional Africa, a survival value in the world of human affairs. Myth provides a counter to the dispossession from time and a stay against time's acceleration.

In the New World, the attempts to eradicate African culture were far more coercive than in Colonial West Africa. The slave master embodied the profane ownership of Western linear time. Though many slave owners were undoubtedly religious and through the windows of Christian ritual had access to sacred, mythic time, their slaves were largely excluded from Christianity until well into the eighteenth century, when conversion was introduced primarily as a further means of obtaining slave obedience. For the two previous centuries, the slave master had viewed his relationship to slaves in a predominantly profane context. This was how, as Gunnar Myrdahl has pointed out, he justified "the peculiar institution": slaves had no souls and were therefore not human and were therefore excluded from the

23. Ibid., p. 276.

spiritual Christian brotherhood. (By the late eighteenth century, slaves had legally become four-fifths human.) This separation of slavery from Christianity meant that the slave master behaved toward the slave as though he (the slave master) were a man without any spiritual alliance. Thus, in an ironic reciprocity, the slave may well have perceived his owner as a man without a soul.

The extended secular status of slavery meant that as an institution it reflected the European attitude toward the New World, divorced from any religious modification of this attitude. The New World was a place of new fortunes, new hope, new identity, where new ideas could be put into practice with minimal impediment. The past could be scuttled. The New World was the territory of the rugged individualist, the self-made man, liberated from the outmoded constraints of European government, church, and family, a territory of total possibility.

It was within this secular context that the slave owner became the archetypal owner of time. As an owner of time, he could own slaves, upon whom he imposed both the concept and the consequences of ownership but to whom he denied the right of ownership. His physical enslavement of the slave was axiomatically equivalent to his enslavement of time. Had the slave master had his way, the result would have been the imposition of timelessness on all his slaves—not in the sense of Western transcendence but in the sense of total dispossession, as in the pennilessness of bankruptcy.

It is important to realize, however, that the slave master did not entirely have his way. The removal of the slave from traditional West African culture was neither immediate nor absolute; as with any migration of great numbers of a people, cultural change was evolutionary, and in the case of the slave radical change was impeded by the racial barriers to his assimilation into New World culture.

The popular view of black slaves in the New World presents a twofold and contradictory image. On the one hand, the slave (seen to possess no cultural tradition of his own) was immediately overwhelmed by the culture of the dominant white man; on the other hand, he remained, as he had always been, a savage impervious to the enlightenment of the West. Neither image is accurate. That slaves were not passive victims is indicated in various forms of rebellion against slavery; moreover, the picture of the cultureless savage being patently inaccurate, the slave community found various ways to nurture certain central aspects of traditional West African culture.

First, there was the centuries-long resistance to slavery itself, a resistance that ended only with emancipation and that foreshadowed the African struggle against colonialism. As outlined by John Hope Franklin, the slave's resistance to his status included escape, revolt, theft, destruction of crops and machinery, working as little as possible, and a guile that often gained what direct resistance would not. John Blassingame asserts that "there is overwhelming evidence in the primary sources . . . of the Negro's resistance to his bondage and of his undying love for freedom." He goes on to cite the "best objective evidence we have" on slave dissatisfaction, Helen T. Catterall's five-volume *Judicial Cases Concerning American Slavery and the Negro*, which shows that "hundreds of slaves sued for their freedom, ran away from their masters, assaulted, robbed, poisoned and murdered whites, burned their masters' dwellings, and committed suicide."[24]

Even a small sample of the available statistics presents a picture of frequent slave rebellion. On shipboard alone, under closely guarded conditions of physical deprivation, there was a slave revolt nearly every other year between 1699 and 1845. In Haiti, the first slave revolt occurred in 1522, twelve years after the first slaves arrived. In the North American colonies, slave revolts occurred on an average of every two years during the two centuries that preceded emancipation in 1863. In Brazil escaped slaves formed a new community that at one time numbered thirty thousand inhabitants before "repacification" by the Portuguese. The Maroon community of Jamaica was formed from the 1655 rebellion; never re-enslaved, descendants of the original rebels still live in the Cockpit Hill Country of the Jamaican

24. John Hope Franklin, *From Slavery to Freedom*, pp. 205ff; John Blassingame, *The Slave Community*, pp. 104–05. The Catterall volumes were published in Washington, D.C., 1926–37.

hinterlands. Though the available data are fragmentary, it seems accurate to conclude, as Herskovits does for example, that over a period of three and one-half centuries, "the tendency to revolt was unremittant."[25]

The widespread incidence of theft by slaves is attested to in the sermons described in the slave narratives collected in the United States during the 1930s. George Rawick, editor of these narratives, points out that the slaves "understood that the official religion was being used as a method of social control and . . . for many slaves it simply did not work."[26] The typical Sunday sermon included admonitions not to steal "missy's chickens and eggs" and to "obey your masters." By inference, Rawick notes, there must have been sufficient theft and disobedience to warrant this habitual commentary. No less a moralist than Booker T. Washington defends the practice of theft in his autobiography, asserting that it was justified by the immorality of slavery.

The resistance to slavery suggests a sense of community among New World slaves, which the slave narratives themselves confirm. Only within the context of a community could the remnants of a traditional African heritage be fostered and retained—and, along with it, a traditional cyclic concept of time.

Though slave owners tried to separate slaves of the same tribal origin, they were often thwarted. According to Blassingame, most plantations required twenty or more slaves, making such separation impossible, as most slaves were taken from the relatively small Guinea Coast area. Though the newly arrived slave might cast about in vain for a member of his own tribal group, he was nevertheless surrounded by others whose customs, social structure, and language were broadly similar. As Raboteau points out, "Similar modes of perception, shared basic principles, and common patterns of ritual were widespread among different West African religions."[27] Furthermore, migrations on the continent of Africa itself resulted in substantial cultural interchange among groups whose customs differed. In sum, the

---

25. Melville Herskovits, *The Myth of the Negro Past*, pp. 91ff.
26. George P. Rawick, *From Sundown to Sunup*, p. 36.
27. Albert J. Raboteau, *Slave Religion*, p. 7.

basis for community existed among people of various tribal origins, all of whom had in common a heritage in which life without a sense of communal responsibility was inconceivable. These factors, taken together with their common state of oppression, fostered the kind of communal strength that the slave owner sought to destroy. On the basis of his analysis of the slave narratives, Rawick asserts that "out of the interaction of the men and women who carried a varied African heritage in their minds and memories along with the enslavement of a harsh plantation system based on slave labor, there emerged over time an independent black community [that] showed the marks of the African experience."[28]

Within the context of this community, religious practices similar to those of traditional Africa continued, encouraged by slave exclusion from Christianity for the first two hundred years of their New World experience. As Raboteau suggests, "One of the most durable and adaptable constituents of the slave's culture, linking African past with American present, was his religion."[29] Like other facets of African culture, he goes on, religion was able to survive because it could be adapted to include—as in Africa—elements of Christianity without being obliterated. By the time slaves were introduced to Christianity in large numbers, we can imagine that some traditional practices were well established. The result of Christian conversion, as in Africa, was a religious syncretism in which Christianity coexisted with a diversity of traditional beliefs. Compelled to attend Sunday church service, many slaves also met secretly after dark for services of their own.

Scholars have noted specific Africanisms in slave religion. In the Caribbean especially, there was a syncretism of Roman Catholic saints with an African pantheon of gods; voodoo has a clear relationship to traditional religions of West Africa. Throughout the New World, the practice of conducting religious ceremonies in a sacred grove echoed African practice, as did the use of drumming. Slave folk medicine resembled that of Africa, and

28. Rawick, p. 36.
29. Raboteau, p. 4.

both were closely linked with religion. In accounts of slave conversion experience, the description recurs of a "little white man" very much like Legba, the trickster-messenger god in the Yoruba pantheon, one of whose roles included that of go-between between the world of the gods and spirits and the world of men. The interplay of the sacred and the secular in the community leadership of the black preacher resembles traditional African practice.

If neither rebellion nor resistance was totally successful, they were nevertheless sufficient to bring into question the slave master's ownership of time and with it his capacity to dispossess others. While the slave was in continual confrontation with the barrier at the far end of the interval of passage—the barrier of slavery itself, which cut him off from history—he was also implicitly denying that his heritage prior to enslavement was a void. By celebrating remembered aspects of the African past, whether in religion, medicine, or in music, he again defied the European ownership of time. Symbolically at least, the slave revolt was an attempt to murder history, and the retention of black heritage was the celebration of myth. Together, the two worked as a counterweight to the slave master's attempt to impose temporal dispossession.

In colonial Africa, a rich cultural tradition could absorb and accommodate Western influence. In the New World the same tradition had somewhat the same effect. In the African-European confrontation between myth and history, black time became contingent, a contingency augmented by the acceleration of time in twentieth-century Africa and by the threat of temporal dispossession experienced by black people throughout the world during the past several hundred years. But the contingencies of black time embody not only uncertainty and flux but also resources sufficient to do battle against uncertainty and the threat of dispossession. In large part, black fiction is the portrayal of that battle.

PART 2

VISION IN BLACK FICTION: THEMES AND FORMS

The Chaos of Time

Central to the themes that unite American, Caribbean, and African fiction is the black writer's focus on the chaos of time. This chaos mimes the historical reality that has been described.

At its best, time is simply "indifferent, like ice or snow," as John Grimes notes in *Go Tell It on the Mountain*. At its worst, time becomes a malignant force hostile to human concerns, as it is for the main character in *Things Fall Apart*: after he has sown his first crop, there is an unseasonable drought, followed by untimely rains. The narrative description is simply that "the year went mad" and in Achebe's novel, as elsewhere throughout black fiction, the madness of time breeds barrenness and destruction.

Time accelerates out of control in a mad cycle of birth and decay in Ayi Kwei Armah's *The Beautyful Ones Are Not Yet Born*. This sense of mad acceleration pervades the novel, symbolized clearly in an anecdote that the main character hears from a former teacher:

In Standard Five, one of us, a boy who took a special pleasure in showing us true but unexpected sides of our world, came and showed us his favorite among the weird lot. It was a picture of something the caption called an old manchild. It had been born with all the features of a human baby, but within seven years it had completed the cycle from babyhood to infancy to youth, to maturity and old age, and in its seventh year it had died a

natural death. The picture [he] showed us was of the manchild in its
gray old age, completely old in everything save the smallness of its size,
a thing that deepened the element of the grotesque. The manchild
looked more irretrievably old, far more thoroughly decayed, than any
ordinary old man could ever have looked [p. 73].

The anecdote provides an image of what Updike has termed the
"synopsis of history" in contemporary Africa, in which time has
accelerated rapidly. But in *The Beautyful Ones* acceleration assumes the flavor of evil, the central antagonist to the main character's survival and spiritual well-being.

Much the same sense of acceleration is apparent at the climax
of Ellison's *Invisible Man*. The battle royal, the adventures
involving Mr. Norton, the job in the paint factory, the concluding riot in Harlem—each episode begins slowly, but the tempo
accelerates to a symbolic explosion of time, figured in images of
electric shock, brawling, an "explosion," and finally a riot. During each episode, the central character goes from optimism and
an illusory sense of control to a realization that he is time's fool,
the victim of a world in which time repeatedly accelerates into
madness.

Time may fragment into an insane discontinuity, as it does in
Lamming's *In the Castle of My Skin*. By the novel's end, Pa, who
earlier has affirmed the essential continuum of cyclic time, has
lost his vision of time's wholeness in the awareness of the chaotic
reality. The fragmentation of time both literally and symbolically sends Pa and his vision to the poorhouse.

Pa represents a character type that recurs throughout black
fiction, a Keeper of Time whose demise (by various means)
symbolizes the disintegration of time into chaos. In Attaway's
Blood on the Forge, for example, the oldest employee at the mill,
whose job is that of timekeeper, represents a certain continuity
between present and past. Toward the end of the novel he is
killed in a mill explosion, his body blown into unrecognizable
fragments. Symbolically, time has exploded, and in a pathetic effort to mend time his fellow employees work his bodily fragments into watch fobs.

In Armah's *Fragments*, the Keeper of Time is Nana, the blind
grandmother, who views time and life in the terms of a tradi-

tional cyclic order: "Death . . . now I see in it another birth, just
as among you [the ancestral spirits] the birth of an infant here is
mourned as the traveling of another spirit" (p. 286). As the narrative proceeds, her voice and her vision are increasingly ignored. By the conclusion of the novel, she is alone, near death,
"a stranger unable to find a home in a town of strangers" (p.
279). The ordered continuity of time that she affirms will, with
her imminent death, also die.

In *The Interpreters*, by Wole Soyinka, the Keeper of Time is the
stutterer Sekoni, a young Nigerian engineer. During his voyage
home from studies in Britain, he dreams of the bridges he will
build, and as the narrative continues it becomes clear that the
bridges in his dreams are symbolic: in an argument, he asserts
that to regard death as final is to "disrupt the dddome of
cccontinuity, which is what life is. . . . We must accccccept the universal dddome, bbbecause there is no dddirection. The bbbridge
is the dddome of rreligion and bbbridges dddon't jjjust gggo
from hhere to ththere; a bridge also faces backward" (p. 9).
Sekoni's stammer ironically fragments the utterance in which he
affirms the traditional African continuity of time, a continuity
between the world of men and the world of spirits, between the
world of the present and that of the past. Midway through *The
Interpreters*, Sekoni meets a violent death. During an unseason-
ably rainy July night, in which the weather is described in images
of a mocking sky-bull divinity "hungry for the blood of earth-
dwellers," "The Dome cracked above Sekoni's short-sighted
head. . . . Too late he saw the insanity of a lorry parked right in
his path, a swerve turned into a skid and cruel arabesque of
tyres. A futile heap of metal, and Sekoni's body lay surprised
across the open door, showers of laminated glass around him,
his beard one fastness of blood and wet earth" (p. 155). The season gone mad, time gone awry—these are the attendants on
Sekoni's collision with a lorry, as the madness of natural process
and time are linked with spiritual destruction and the Keeper of
Time dies.

Throughout black fiction, the death of the continuity of time
constitutes a spiritual loss. Perhaps the clearest illustration of
how time relates to spirit comes in Achebe's *Arrow of God*, in

which Ezeulu, the main character, is a traditional priest whose community responsibility is to mark the passage of the seasons, to act as the Keeper of Time. In the symbolic progression of the novel, Ezeulu loses his vision of cyclic continuity and attempts to become the individual owner of time. By the conclusion, British missionaries and colonial personnel have eroded the traditional sacred stability of the village and Ezeulu has lapsed into madness, his death imminent. But whether in traditional Africa or the New World twentieth century, the death of the Keeper of Time in black fiction signals a death of the spirit whose effect is felt throughout the world portrayed.

Bigger Thomas, in *Native Son*, gives a name to the landscape that is void of a Keeper of Time. During the course of the narrative, he sees himself as inhabiting a "shadowy region . . . a No Man's Land, the ground that separates the white world from the black world," a place where he feels "naked, transparent" (p. 68). Bigger's past is a blank, largely ignored in Wright's narrative; his future is a prison cell and ultimately execution. Cut off from time, Bigger and the world he inhabits mime the realities of history: like his slave and colonial counterparts, he dwells in the uncertain flux that characterizes the interval of passage between myth and history, inhabiting neither, cut off from both. Recalling the figure given in Part 1 clarifies the qualities of the landscape that Bigger calls No Man's Land:

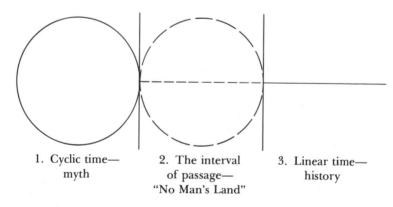

1. Cyclic time—   2. The interval   3. Linear time—
      myth   of passage—   history
                        "No Man's Land"

Figure 4

The interval of passage is at once the place of temporal chaos and of temporal dispossession, where Bigger Thomas is fixed in a state of timeless estrangement. For Bigger, as for the other residents of this landscape, living in No Man's Land is tantamount to spiritual and/or physical death, where the isolation in time coincides with an isolation from the human community.

Historically, Bigger's No Man's Land is a part of the Georgia landscape described by W. E. B. DuBois in *The Souls of Black Folk*. After discussing "physical, economic, and political relations of Negroes and whites in the South," DuBois goes on to describe the state of "spiritual turmoil" that accompanies these relations, which may at first not be apparent to the visitor:

The casual observer visiting the South sees at first little. . . . But if he lingers long enough there comes the awakening. . . . Slowly but surely his eyes begin to catch the shadows of the color-line: here he meets crowds of Negroes and whites; then he is suddenly aware that he cannot discover a single dark face; or again . . . he may find himself in some strange assembly, where all faces are tinged brown or black. . . . He realizes at last that silently, resistlessly, the world about flows by him in two great streams: they ripple on in the same sunshine, they approach and mingle their waters in seeming carelessness,—then they divide and flow wide apart. It is done quietly; no mistakes are made, or if one occurs, the wide arm of the law and of public opinion swings down for a moment, as when the other day a black man and a white woman were arrested for talking together on Whitehall Street in Atlanta[1]

No Man's Land occurs at the confluence of the "two great streams," a confluence whose turmoil embodies the uncertain temporal flux that has been described and whose consequences may be far graver than the arrest suffered by the Atlanta couple.

The destructiveness of No Man's Land shapes the common experience of black characters in fiction. Occasionally, though, a white character ventures into its domain and, like the white woman in DuBois's description, becomes as vulnerable to "arrest" as those who are black. Becky, in Jean Toomer's story of that name, is the archetypal white victim of its destructiveness. The mother of two black sons, she lives in a house "islandized" between the railroad track and the highway, their twin barriers

1. W. E. B. DuBois, *The Souls of Black Folk*, pp. 332–33.

miming the barriers that cut No Man's Land off from both the past and the future. Her isolation is absolute; people have not seen her for years, and they know she exists only because they see her two boys from time to time, mostly engaged in causing trouble. Becky experiences a fate equivalent to Bigger's. Her sons leave town and the community knows she is still alive only by the wisps of smoke issuing from the chimney of her house; later, they learn she has died when the chimney crumbles and her house collapses inward. In circumstances and fate, Becky is Bigger's white counterpart, isolated in both time and space, from heritage as well as community, her destruction arising from the dispossession endemic throughout No Man's Land.

The white hermit in William Demby's *Beetlecreek* is similarly destroyed. His shack is "islandized" between the white part of town and the black, and he is befriended by a young black boy who has come from out of town to visit relatives. Like Becky, isolated, his only human connection is with a black child. In the end, the boy—like Becky's sons—leaves; and the "nigger lover" is killed by a gang of white boys.

Mary, Bigger's victim in *Native Son*, is another inhabitant of No Man's Land; and her death symbolically prefigures Bigger's own. She persuades Bigger to take her and her boyfriend to a restaurant in black Chicago and in so doing enters a territory that embodies dispossession. The moment she crosses the boundary her death is implicit, and she joins Toomer's Becky, Demby's hermit, and Bigger as a casualty of dispossession.

For the black character, No Man's Land is either the area of his beginning or a region he enters, either through blindness or necessity. (The exception is the character whose world is that of traditional Africa, in which the cyclic continuum is still intact—for example, the traditional Akan society of *A Woman in Her Prime*. Within this setting, Asare Konadu charts the efforts of a barren woman to conceive a child. Her struggle, to be sure, is to maintain the cyclic continuum; but it takes place in a world whose concept of time has not been brought into question.) For the majority of black characters, however, the temporal chaos of No Man's Land is the place where their strength and insight are tried. Bigger begins and ends there.

Many characters in black fiction attempt to escape their past, to flee from time. This happens, for example, in the American "passing" novel, a genre popular early in this century. The typical fate of the black character who attempts to pass is that his past catches up with him, often in the melodramatic birth of a black child. Symbolically, passing is an attempt to flee No Man's Land by repudiating the past; the revelation embodied in the black child proves the impossibility of this repudiation. Much the same is true throughout black fiction: the character who flees his past finds that it has pursued him. At best, he realizes that the price is extraordinarily high, the gain insignificant.

When the African novelist portrays the futility implicit in these attempts at flight, he accomplishes two things: he counters the stereotyped image of Africa as the place where time is lost, and obliquely affirms the continuum of time in charting the futility, often the destruction, that attends those who deny it.

Juana, in Armah's *Fragments*, is a Puerto Rican psychiatrist whose sojourn in Ghana is an attempt to flee the past. She has a New World belief in the linearity of new beginnings, but ironically finds only the recapitulation of her previous life. She comes to Ghana to escape a sense of futility, "prepared to find her own part in a struggle assumed to be going on." But she finds no struggle, "none of the fire of defiance; just the living defeat of whole peoples." And in this defeat she finds "the familiar fabric of her life" (p. 45). The human destructiveness she encounters in Africa is equivalent to that in the world she has left behind.

An episode in Achebe's *No Longer at Ease* touches on much the same idea. Two Irish teachers in a Roman Catholic mission school have come to Africa to escape the boredom of home. In the company of the main character of the novel, Obi, and one of his friends, they attempt to "explore" Nigeria by eating Nigerian food, learning some Ibo words, and dancing to African highlife music. But their effort is abruptly curtailed by the strictures of a Mother Superior who, bent on maintaining the mores of home, forbids any further acquaintance with Obi. Achebe takes leave of the two girls alone in their room, sipping tea, their Africa constricted to a daily round much like the one they have left behind in Ireland. Similarly, Monica Faseyi, the British wife of a Nigerian physician in *The Interpreters*, enjoys the Africanness of Africa—its palm wine, its highlife music, its departures from the customs of home. But she finds that the Nigerian social set in which her husband moves is bent on adopting British social trappings: she must wear gloves, drink gin, and listen to Tchaikovsky.

Joe Golder, a black American professor of history in *The Interpreters*, journeys to Nigeria in retreat from the ambiguities of being black in a predominantly white culture, in search of a "lost birthright." Ironically, he finds himself being mistaken again and again for a white person (he is one-fourth black and light in complexion). No longer black in a white society, he is white in a black one, and the shift in terms creates an equivalent ambiguity.

Juana, Joe Golder, and the two Irish teachers are not African: they are seeking in Africa an escape from home and the past. But, in contrast to Conrad's Kurtz or Bellow's Henderson, they are pursued by that which they sought to leave behind. In the hands of the African novelist, their fate is an ironic affirmation of the continuity of time.

For the African character who seeks escape from his traditional past, arduous struggle leads him to the temporal chaos of No Man's Land. Achebe's Obi, in *No Longer at Ease*, is the archetype. As a child Obi was discouraged by his father from associating with the "heathens" in his village. After a college education in England, the rejection of the traditional world of his grandfather (Okonkwo of *Things Fall Apart*) is complete. He admires Graham Greene's *Heart of the Matter* and considers Scobie's suicide a "happy ending." Suicide was abomination in Okonkwo's traditional society; it was also his chosen death. That Obi can see suicide as a happy ending is an index to his estrangement from his African past as well as that of his own family.

This estrangement is also reflected in a poem Obi writes about Nigeria:

> How sweet it is to lie beneath a tree
> At eventime and share the ecstasy
> Of jocund birds and flimsy butterflies
> How sweet to leave our earthbound body in its mud,

> And rise towards the music of the spheres,
> Descending softly with the wind,
> And the tender glow of the fading sun.   [p. 23]

Obi later calls the poem "callow" and "nostalgic," but it is worse than that. In its prosody, its sentimentality, its view of nature, and its denigration of the "earthbound" body it not only contradicts his Ibo heritage but is at best a cheap imitation of an adolescent European lyricism. One could better understand and sympathize with Obi's denial of his heritage if he were able to find something worthwhile to replace it. Like the magi in Eliot's poem, Obi is "no longer at ease in the old dispensation." But whereas Eliot's poem leaves the reader with the feeling that the distress of the magi is a necessary price for the vision they have experienced, there is little apparent gain on Obi's part beyond a certain glib facility at making allusions to English literature and writing imitative poetry.

Obi's relationship with Clara charts further implications of rejecting the past, implications not only for Obi but for his parents as well. According to Ibo custom Obi's planned marriage to Clara, an *osu* (the descendant of a slave caste of traditional Iboland), would be taboo. Having rejected such strictures, Obi is determined to marry the woman he loves. His parents, however, are horrified, even though they have been practicing Christians most of their lives. Obi's mother threatens to commit suicide, and his father compares marriage to an *osu* with marriage to a leper. Obi returns to Clara and tells her that they must wait awhile. The problem is dramatically, perhaps melodramatically, heightened because Clara is pregnant. Obi acquiesces to her decision to have an abortion at the hands of the businesslike doctor who asks "thirty pounds hard cash" (p. 137). Following the abortion, Clara vanishes from Obi's life, and he makes no determined effort to find her.

Having rejected traditional sanctions, neither Obi nor his parents are able to live up to their adopted European, Christian ideals. Obi's parents simultaneously reject and cling to a belief about *osus* that belongs to the past. From the point of view of the traditional Umuofia of Obi's grandparents, the abortion is an abomination. The landscape that Obi at this point surveys is that of No Man's Land. Having attempted to reject the past, he finds that it pursues him in his parents' rejection of Clara. Though he is no longer at ease with the old dispensation, it nevertheless shapes his life. This is shown again in the aftermath of the abortion: he loses Clara—his "future"—as well.

In *The Interpreters* the Oguazors, the leaders of the social set that Monica Faseyi finds so disappointingly un-African, reject their African past and decorate their homes with bowls of plastic apples and other European fruit. Sagoe calls it the "house of deaths," after reaching for an apple to eat and discovering that it is fake. With a delighted Monica Faseyi, Sagoe then dances a highlife to *Swan Lake*, throws numerous pieces of the plastic fruit out the window to a nonexistent dog, then goes outside and throws them in again. Professor Oguazor, whose stiff bow, stilted British accent, and equally stilted values are "from the marionette pages of Victoriana," more than deserves Sagoe. Here, the consequence of rejecting the past is to become the deserved object of ridicule.

But there is a darker side to the satirization of the Oguazors. Professor Oguazor has a daughter by his housemaid, the "plastic apple of his eye"; but, hypocritically, he keeps her hidden away while at the same time denouncing one of his unmarried students' pregnancy as "meral turpitude [*sic*]." The reader, but not Oguazor, knows that Egbo (a friend of Sagoe's) is responsible for the pregnancy; a pregnancy that Soyinka portrays as symbolically sacred. Egbo is shown as allied with Ogun, a traditional Yoruba god; he has a "shrine" to the god, a hidden rock pool on the River Ogun. Soyinka's emphasis on the sacredness of this site is clear in the description of Egbo's feelings when he awakens after spending his first night there:

Egbo rose and looked around him, bathing and wondering at life, for it seemed to him that he was born again, he felt night now as a womb of the gods and a passage for travellers. . . . He left with a gift he could not define upon his body, for what traveller beards the gods in their den and departs without a divine boon? [p. 27]

This shrine is where Egbo and the girl picnic and then make love, the consequence of which Oguazor denounces as a sign of "meral turpitude." In symbolic terms, Oguazor condemns the offspring of a sacred union, one that celebrates past values and thus embodies a temporal continuity much like that expressed in Sekoni's metaphor of the bridge between past and present. For this hypocritical condemnation of the unmarried girl, Oguazor is cursed in words that also embody traditional values: "I hope you live to bury your daughters" (p. 250). The harshness of this curse, made by another friend of Egbo's, demands a mythic justice, a sacrificial demand of a death for the denial of life.

The Interpreters ends shortly thereafter, the curse left unfulfilled. But in *Fragments* Armah describes a similar situation in which an implied curse is fulfilled. A young woman holds an outdooring ceremony (a naming ritual) for her newborn baby prematurely, because the earlier date coincides with payday and therefore promises more generous gifts for the child. In traditional Akan custom a premature outdooring was tantamount to tempting the child to return to the spirit world from which he had just come. Shortly after the ceremony, the child dies, his death the judgment of a heritage.

In African fiction, the consequences of the attempt to escape from the past are clear: Obi finds himself in No Man's Land; Oguazor is ridiculed and cursed; a young woman loses her child. In Caribbean writer Orlando Patterson's *Children of Sisyphus*, the consequence is even harsher. Dinah, the central character, begins in No Man's Land, a Jamaican slum called the Dungle that lies between Kingston proper and the sea, a community of packing-box houses built upon a human wastefill. Dinah's hope is to escape the Dungle, and thus her past; but each step she takes away from it leads her inexorably back. Her return to the Dungle manifests the fatality of cyclic recurrence, the *ogbanje* cycle of traditional African society; and in her death, the destructiveness of this cycle is made clear.

Dinah supports her husband, Cyrus, by becoming a prostitute. In an attempt to better her life, she leaves the Dungle and Cyrus for Jonestown, a less poverty-stricken area, where she is kept for a time by a former client whom she loathes. When she learns that a neighbor has cast an *obeah* spell on her, intended to take her back to the Dungle, she flees again, leaving her former client to work as a housemaid and turning for advice to Father Shephard, leader of a religious cult. She becomes Shephard's consecrated mate, making the "Elder Mother" who funds Shephard's work jealous. On the eve of Shephard and Dinah's planned departure for England, the Elder Mother short-circuits the lights in the church, kills Shephard with a butcher knife, and thrusts the knife into Dinah's hand. Shephard's congregation attacks Dinah, wounding her badly before she is rescued and taken away by Sammy, a garbageman. But she flees from Sammy in turn and dies just as she reaches the Dungle and the arms of Cyrus. The Dungle, like the blighted *ogbanje* cycle of traditional culture, is not to be escaped, a doom announced in the novel's title and confirmed in Dinah's tale.

The theme of the futility of repudiating the past and No Man's Land recurs throughout black fiction. James Baldwin uses it again and again. Gabriel Grimes, in *Go Tell It on the Mountain*, is in perpetual, conscious flight from time as he twice repudiates his past only to find that it has pursued him. He begins his manhood as a liquor-drinking womanizer. Seized by a Saul-of-Tarsus-like conversion to Christianity, he becomes a preacher and marries Deborah, the "holy fool" victim of a white gang rape, who is frigid and barren as a result. In his ministry and in his marriage, Gabriel seeks a shield against his past, but finds only its recapitulation when he encounters Esther, who in his eyes is a gin-drinking temptress. After Gabriel gets her pregnant Esther leaves for the North, financing the trip with coins from Deborah's sugar bowl, and later dies in childbirth. The son she bears Gabriel, Royal, will later be killed in a knife fight.

Deborah dies, and Gabriel goes North. Once again, the pattern of his life is repeated. His first son with his new wife (the "second" Royal) not only carries the same name as his son by Esther but also experiences the same fate. Injured in a knife fight, he is beaten by Gabriel, whose purpose is clearly not only punishment but exorcism of a past that he cannot escape. This sense of recapitulation is strengthened by the illegitimate son that Gabriel's new wife brings into their marriage, the illegitimacy an echo of the first Royal's circumstance.

Gabriel's sister, Florence, also chooses No Man's Land, thinking of it as a place where one rids oneself of past shame. Like Gabriel, she flees the South, afraid that it will "swallow up her future." She bleaches her skin, straightens her hair, and marries a man who she thinks will shield her from the poverty she experienced in her past; but by the end of the novel her husband has deserted her and, childless and poor, she lives alone in a grubby room, dying in pain from cancer. Like Gabriel, she has sought to better herself by escaping her past, but ironically it is her fear of the past that has "swallowed up" her future.

In Ellison's *Invisible Man*, the central character's state of continual flight fulfills the curse he dreams about early in the novel: at a circus with his grandfather, he opens an envelope that should contain a scholarship to a Negro college, his ticket to the future; but he finds instead "an engraved document containing a short message in letters of gold," which says "To Whom It May Concern . . . Keep This Nigger Boy Running" (p. 26). His story chronicles his race toward his future and his belief in the linearity of new beginnings; simultaneously, it charts the ways in which his past shame pursues him, repeatedly metamorphosing the new into a recapitulation of the old. In his final flight during the riot that concludes the novel, he carries with him the briefcase containing the emblems of this past shame—Mary's Black Sambo piggy bank, Tod Clifton's dancing doll, Brother Tarp's link of chain, Jack's letter of betrayal, and all the rest. As he takes up his underground residence, he realizes that his flight has been one of cyclic futility and that "the end was in the beginning" (p. 431).

Similarly, in Achebe's *Things Fall Apart*, Okonkwo, the son of an indolent father, predicates his entire life on the necessity to escape the shame of his father's failure. But by the novel's end he has ironically recapitulated in suicide the shame and the abomination embodied in his father's life and death.

In sum, No Man's Land is a place of chaos, in which time may explode at any moment, where one is constantly threatened with dispossession from time; a landscape that is nevertheless not to be escaped. For many characters in black fiction, it is their permanent dwelling place. Its lethal quality is perhaps best summed up in what happens to sexuality in this world.

In traditional Africa, sexuality was inextricable from procreation, and embodied the continuum of the sacred cycle. In *No Longer at Ease*, *Fragments*, and *The Interpreters*, Clara's abortion, the newborn child's death, and the Oguazors' attitude toward pregnancy signal the unfortunate disruption of time in No Man's Land. In other novels, disruption becomes perversion. In *Native Son*, sexuality is linked with rape and murder. In Attaway's *Blood on the Forge*, a prostitute with a rotted-away breast symbolizes the steel-mill community. In McKay's *Banana Bottom*, a Jamaican character who rejects his black past copulates with a goat. Deborah, in *Go Tell It on the Mountain*, is barren as the result of a white gang rape. In Gayl Jones's *Corregidora*, the main character's grandmother and mother have both been fathered by the same Portuguese slave master. In *Invisible Man*, Jim Trueblood fathers children by both his wife and his daughter. Throughout black fiction, sexual disruption and perversion are images of the larger fragmentation and perversion of the continuum of time.

Though Richard Wright has given a name to this landscape, certain qualities of No Man's Land are familiar in West African folklore, specifically in the tales centering on Ananse, the trickster-spider who when he crossed the Atlantic was reborn as Brer Rabbit.

In one story, for example, Ananse rebels against famine by "dying"—first making certain that his wife will "bury" him above ground. At night, when his family is asleep, Ananse secretly cooks and eats his fill. He eventually meets his comeuppance—in the West African version at the hands of the Gum Man; as Brer Rabbit, at the hands of Tar Baby. Until the trick is revealed, Ananse is an inhabitant of No Man's Land, cut off from both time and the community, existing outside of them: neither alive nor dead, he has sacrificed his heritage to gain a full stomach. Throughout black fiction, characters who choose a similar sacrifice of heritage recur—the Oguazors, the young mother in *Fragments*, Obi, a number of characters in *Invisible Man* and novels by James Baldwin, and innumerable others. Like Ananse, they choose dispossession for the sake of material gain, a full stomach. Ananse disguises himself as dead, but in spiritual terms the disguise is the reality; and much the same death is implied in the various disguises adopted by characters in black fiction. The disguise is chosen for the purpose of personal, material gain; typically the price for this gain is the loss of one's identity, as the disguise becomes reality. Rinehart in *Invisible Man* is the archetype: pimp, preacher, numbers tycoon, the man of many disguises becomes an Ananse figure whose only reality is the sum of the illusions he creates. As a trickster, he gains money and power, but his fragmentation makes a mockery of any notion of temporal continuity. The difference between Ananse's story and Rinehart's lies not in their persons but in the respective worlds they inhabit: Ananse's disguise is at odds with a world in which time is sacred and continuous; Rinehart's fragmentation is at one with the temporal chaos of No Man's Land. But the spiritual loss that each embodies is equivalent.

A variation on Ananse is offered by the "passing" novel, in which a character's repudiation of color implies a rejection of heritage and a spiritual loss equivalent to Rinehart's. Rena Walden, in *The House Behind the Cedars* (Chesnutt, 1900), is an example. The daughter of a white man and his black mistress, she decides to pass for white, only to have her deception revealed just as she is about to marry. Like Ananse, she is exposed, but for Rena, the consequences are more severe: after attempts by both her black employer and her white fiancé to exploit her sexually, she dies, her repudiation of heritage and its implied spiritual loss followed closely by her sexual degradation and death. In James Weldon Johnson's *Autobiography of an Ex-Colored Man*, the consequences of passing are portrayed somewhat less melodramatically: the main character is fortunate enough to maintain his disguise, but he acknowledges the spiritual price of his success in the closing lines of his narrative, asserting that he has "sold his birthright for a mess of pottage."

One of the more complex portrayals of Ananse—aside from the folk figure, perhaps the earliest—is offered in the stories that comprise *The Conjure Woman*. Uncle Julius, Chesnutt's black narrator-protagonist (there is also a white narrator-protagonist, Uncle Julius's employer), uses guile in combination with stories of antebellum conjuration to gain his own ends—whether to persuade his northern employer to buy a worthless horse rather than the intended mule, or to gain the use of an abandoned building for a church. In turn, however, Chesnutt uses Uncle Julius and his stories to indict the post-Reconstruction northern liberal along with the antebellum Southerner, for Chesnutt— like Uncle Julius—plays the role of Ananse, using guile where more direct means might well have proven futile. The effectiveness of Chesnutt's Ananse-like stance is underscored when the stories (published separately in *Atlantic Monthly* beginning in 1887) are seen within their historical context.

In many ways, the period when Chesnutt began publishing these stories was the nadir of the black human condition in the United States, as John Hope Franklin, for example, has pointed out:

The last quarter of the nineteenth century witnessed the steady deterioration of the position of Negroes in the United States. The end of Reconstruction had left them without any protection from the merciless attacks of the Klan and other terrorist groups who continued to use the mythical threat of "Negro rule" as their excuse for lawlessness. A few Negroes still voted, but they did so at great peril; and the numbers declined with every passing year.

Educational opportunities for Negroes were quite limited, with segregated schools in the South suffering from wanton discrimination in the allocation of public funds and with struggling denominational schools inadequately supported by their Northern benefactors. Negroes had little economic security, moreover. In the South the new industries were closed to them; and most were forced to subsist as small farmers or hapless sharecroppers. In the North new labor unions barred them from membership, while "new" immigrants showed their hostility in a variety of ways.[2]

In this historical milieu Chesnutt's voice was initially a lonely one: in 1887, DuBois was still at Fisk University, publishing only in the student publication, *The Herald*;[3] and only three full-length works of fiction had been published in the United States by black writers.[4] And if black voices had been largely stifled,

2. John Hope Franklin, Introduction to *Three Negro Classics*, p. vii.
3. Ibid., p. xii.
4. Robert Bone, The *Negro Novel in America*, pp. 258–59.

white writers had found a highly popular and lucrative genre in
the plantation novel, in which the black slave was alternately
portrayed as possessed of "the happy mentality of puppies" or as
"a primitive savage, capable of any crime or violence."[5] Thus,
both social conditions and publishing preferences stacked the
odds against a militant voice in black fiction.

Moreover, the periodical that first agreed to publish Chesnutt, *Atlantic Monthly*, was itself a bastion of the Genteel Tradition. John Tomsich points out in *The Genteel Endeavor* that
during the 1880s the *Atlantic* had a reputation as the "best-edited
journal in the English-speaking world," but it was also "among
the more timid."[6] As editor, Thomas Bailey Aldrich vetoed the
inclusion of any controversial political or economic material and,
perhaps because his readership comprised "mainly middle class
women," he held firm to an editorial policy based on the
virginibus maxim (print nothing offensive to virgins).[7]

To appreciate Uncle Julius's (and Chesnutt's) voice, one must
hear it ringing out within the context of the multiple hostilities
that have been described. Keeping this context in mind while ex-
amining "Mars Jeems's Nightmare," for example, demonstrates
both the complexity and the survival capacity of the Ananse
figure.

In "Mars Jeems's Nightmare," Uncle Julius's white employer
has decided to fire Uncle Julius's grandson for incompetence.
Uncle Julius tells him a story about how Mars Jeems, a slave
owner of antebellum North Carolina, was turned into a slave,
through conjuration, because he was too harsh toward the slaves
he owned, especially a slave named Solomon. After this experience, according to Uncle Julius, Mars Jeems reformed and
treated his slaves with consideration, even sending a buggy to
fetch Solomon's betrothed from a neighboring plantation. After
hearing Uncle Julius's story, Annie, the Northerner's wife,
agrees to give the grandson one more chance.

In the story told by Uncle Julius, Solomon is an Ananse
figure: angered by the harsh treatment he has been receiving

5. Ibid., p. 22.
6. John Tomsich, *The Genteel Endeavor*, p. 22.
7. Ibid., p. 120.

and by the forced separation from his betrothed, he chooses secret conjuration rather than open rebellion as a weapon against
his white master. At his behest, Aunt Peggy conjures Mars
Jeems, the result of which is that Solomon gains what he could
not win by direct rebellion, as Mars Jeems gains a firsthand experience of No Man's Land. Uncle Julius gains as much as Solomon, whose story also softens Annie's heart sufficiently to win
another chance for Uncle Julius's grandson.

Finally, Charles Chesnutt himself can best be understood as
an Ananse figure. Using the format of the plantation story
made popular by white writers, he published stories that sought
to evoke sympathy for slaves rather than ridicule. In the super-
stitious darky Uncle Julius he created a character who not only
entertained in the best minstrel tradition but who also, in the
best tradition of the didactic African folk tale, instructed his audience in the proper mode of moral rectitude. And it is surely no
accident that Annie, the Northerner's wife in *The Conjure
Woman*, is the fictional analogue of the predominantly white
middle-class readership of the *Atlantic*. One may imagine the
readership identifying with Annie and therefore perhaps extending into real life Annie's sympathy and understanding of
the black human condition.

Adroitly, then, Chesnutt has woven a plantation tale in which
militance assumes the guise of minstrelsy without losing sight of
its purpose: as Solomon gets back his betrothed and Uncle Julius
gets back his grandson's job, Chesnutt offers a portrait of black
character that at least obliquely gives the lie to the plantation
novel stereotype. For Chesnutt, as for the characters he
portrays, the Ananse disguise is unquestionably effective. Moreover, in the conjunction of Solomon, Uncle Julius, and Charles
Chesnutt, there emerges an implicit continuity of heritage—and
tentatively at least the redemption of Ananse into time.

There are certain differences between the Ananse of black
fiction and his folk counterpart, differences that in large part
arise from a difference in circumstance. First, though the
fictional Ananse has as much to gain from the successful use of
guile and disguise—in some instances, survival itself—he has less
to lose in spiritual terms: in the temporal chaos of No Man's

Land, he *begins* in a state of dispossession, which his role as Ananse merely confirms. Second, the fictional Ananse typically fits his role to white expectation—for example, when Bledsoe in *Invisible Man* advises the central character to "show the white folks what they want to see." The catch is that the "white folks" themselves may impose a disguise that serves their own purposes—the stereotypes of the happy darky, the colored mammy, Uncle Tom, the black rapist. For example, both Tod Clifton and the central character in *Invisible Man* become the black puppets of the Brotherhood in spite of the fact that their sincere intention is to help the black people of Harlem. When Clifton realizes this, breaks with the Brotherhood, and begins selling Black Sambo dancing dolls on the streets of Harlem, his status as an Ananse figure is displayed in the dolls: created by the white world, sold to blacks, the black puppet has lost his soul not for his own gain but for that of the white world. When Clifton embraces death at the hands of the white policeman, his act has been prefigured in his earlier spiritual dispossession.

Even when the fictional character voluntarily chooses an Ananse role, his decision is typically irreversible: the wall barricading the world where time may perpetually be renewed becomes impassable. When the folk figure's trick is revealed, he is again taken in to the community of the living; when the fictional character's status is revealed to himself or to others, his options are more complex and far less certain. Rinehart endures, as does the more sympathetically portrayed Uncle Julius. For those who "pass," the price typically is spiritual and/or physical death. For Tod Clifton, too, revelation has the consequence of death. Only rarely is Ananse redeemed into time, as perhaps happens in *The Conjure Woman* as the result of Chesnutt's sleight of hand.

Were Ananse's choice the only option available in black fiction, the "pottage" that it sometimes wins could perhaps be honored as some recompense for the spiritual dispossession of No Man's Land. But Ananse's choice is not the only one available. Other characters who are neither so devious as Uncle Julius nor as quiescent as Tod Clifton struggle openly against this dispossession. Though, like Clifton, they may ultimately die, they extract a price for their dying.

Vision, Rebellion, and Redemption

In the midst of temporal chaos, against the backdrop of potential despair and the barren landscape of No Man's Land, themes of vision, rebellion, and ultimate redemption counter the bleakness. Black fiction, like black history, is in large measure the chronicle of struggle against the contingencies of time.

One victory belongs to the Keeper of Time, who endures chaos with a clear, though largely impotent, vision of order and continuity. Sometimes he is unable even to share his vision with anyone else. But he has no illusions. He sees the malevolence of time, and he sees also the futility of trying to escape from it. But usually the best he can achieve is a certain day-to-day adjustment of the chaos to a more human dimension.

Egbo's alliance with Ogun in *The Interpreters* exemplifies this vision. Though he is unable to change the Oguazors or the world they represent, vision at least allows him to endure. White writers sometimes portray this quality of vision in the older black woman who takes no nonsense but who comforts and endures. Though the portrayal sometimes degenerates into the Aunt Jemima stereotype, Dilsey in *The Sound and the Fury* maintains both her dignity and her strength as she endures throughout the chaos of generations, knowing that the clocks in the Compson household have gone awry and making the appropriate adjustment wherever she can. She is a figure of strength, the moral norm of Faulkner's novel, a Keeper of Time who is not destroyed by her vision. Dilsey resembles any number of women characters in black fiction—Jane Pittman, Ursa Corregidora's grandmother, Bita Plant, Pilate Dead, DuBois's Zora. In contrast to Dilsey, however, these women share their strength of vision with the black community rather than with a degenerate white southern family. Because the subject of women characters in black fiction is dealt with in depth in a later section, detailed remarks here are confined to only one example, Elizabeth in *Go Tell It on the Mountain*.

Unlike her husband, Gabriel, and her sister-in-law, Florence, Elizabeth does not seek to repudiate her past, though her life, like theirs, has been characterized by loss and hardship. Instead, she celebrates the past in the present. Without denying that her father was a pimp, she celebrates his love for her; without attempting to escape the South, she goes North with Ronny because she loves him. When Ronny commits suicide, leaving Elizabeth pregnant with John, she celebrates her love for the father in her love for the baby. When Gabriel asks her to repent of her "sin," she refuses to be sorry that "she brought Johnny into the world" (p. 184). As Gabriel's wife, too, she embodies a celebration of life, rather than its denial. In the nurturing acceptance of her family—her father, her husband, her children, and the dead Ronny—she is a force of continuity in a world that would, in its repudiation of the past, fragment time. Her favorite Bible verse is "All things work together for good to them that love the Lord." In her vision, the wholeness of love and the wholeness of time work together, making the past of a piece with the present.

The change that Elizabeth's vision effects, drawn by implication only, comes through the example she provides for her son John. At the beginning of his narrative, John Grimes shares Florence and Gabriel's displacement from time. He sees his life as an endless cycle of futility, imaged in a futile struggle against filth:

John hated sweeping this carpet, for dirt rose, clogging his nose and sticking to his sweaty skin, and he felt that should he sweep it forever, the clouds of dust would not diminish, the rug would not be clean. It became in his imagination his impossible, lifelong task, his hard trial, like that of a man he had read about somewhere, whose curse it was to push a boulder up a steep hill, only to have the giant who guarded the hill roll the boulder down again—and so on, forever, throughout eternity. For each dustpan he so laboriously filled at the doorsill demons added to the rug twenty more [pp. 26–27].

John's allusion to Sisyphus and his feeling of having been cursed with cyclic futility echo the circumstance of the main character of Patterson's *Children of Sisyphus*. To the extent that he is the child of his stepfather, Gabriel, John feels the curse of the father visited upon the son. Ultimately, however, unlike Gabriel, he refuses the temptation to flee from this curse, but instead follows Elizabeth's example. By so doing he gains a vision of time's continuity and gains, too, a limited victory.

His refusal of temptation comes in his conversion at the end of the novel. The "voice" that tempts him tells him to "get up from the filthy floor" (using his own image of the cyclic futility of time), and show that he is better than "the other niggers." When John refuses, the voice again tempts him, this time specifically to repudiate Gabriel, arguing that if he is converted to his father's religion he implicitly has acquiesced to the shame that Gabriel sees in him, a curse that he can escape if he gets up "from the filthy floor." John again refuses. The third time, the voice argues that, Gabriel aside, conversion means accepting the continuation of the cyclic curse. After John's final refusal, his conversion culminates in a vision of his oneness with all those who represent his past, his father and mother and "all the despised and rejected, the spat upon, all the earth's offscouring" (p. 201). Though John, like Elizabeth, sees that time is out of joint, that it implies shame, that it in fact represents a No Man's Land, like Elizabeth too he stands his ground, refusing dispossession from the only heritage he has, choosing to celebrate rather than deny. As its title implies, the novel portrays a nativity, the birth of John Grimes's redemptive vision of his heritage, his entry into a fierce alliance with time that counters the chaos of No Man's Land.

Just as Elizabeth's strength bears fruit in John's celebration, so does his conversion move Florence to a vision of time's whole-

ness, a vision that in the closing pages of the novel she attempts
to share with Gabriel. She confronts Gabriel as they leave the
church after John's conversion, telling him that all his life he has
been seeking to "do better" and as a consequence "whatever you
done already, whatever you doing right at that minute, don't
count" (p. 214). She demands, in other words, that he stop frag-
menting the future from the past, insisting with Elizabeth and
with John that they are all of a piece. She ends by threatening
him if he doesn't mend his ways, she will tell Elizabeth that "she
ain't the only sinner in [Gabriel's] holy house" and that "little
Johnny ain't the only bastard" (p. 214). In sum, she confronts
him with his past, demanding that he acknowledge Esther and
his son by her. The hope at the conclusion of the novel is that, if
Gabriel can acknowledge his own illegitimate son—to himself as
well as to Elizabeth—he will in turn be able to accept Johnny. In
accepting his own past, he will symbolically gain a future.

In *Go Tell It on the Mountain*, Elizabeth's vision figures as a catalyst for the vision of others. Similarly, in *The Beautyful Ones Are
Not Yet Born*, the vision of the central character, identified only
as "the man," is initially guided by a former teacher of his who
on a single occasion in the long-ago past experienced a vision of
time's continuity in the endless motion of the sea, movements
"stretching back into ages to very long ago . . . giving the watcher
the childhood feeling of infinite things finally understood" (p.
84). The teacher has lost all but the memory of his vision and has
retreated from the world into the isolation of his house, cutting
himself off from the world of corruption and filth. For the man,
the vision thus initiated deepens and provides succor against
temporal madness, which is symbolized in the anecdote of the
"old manchild" who within the span of seven years completed
the cycle from birth to old age and death. The man works as a
timekeeper for the railroad, his duty to keep the trains running
on schedule. It becomes clear that his job is symbolic, that he is
the Keeper of Time in a chaotic world. Though his vision is
largely incapable of changing this world, he is to be commended
for surviving with his vision intact.

The Beautyful Ones is set in Takoradi, a Ghanaian city whose
spiritual chaos is revealed in images of filth. The man's immedi-

ate task is to maintain his footing as he slips in puddles of vomit, almost collides with the night-soil man, leaps "across yards made up of the mud of days of rain," jumps over "wide gutters with only a trickle of drying urine at the bottom and so many clusters of cigarette pieces wet and pinched in where they have left the still unsatisfied lips of the smoker," and balances precariously on the platform in a public latrine amid "rows of cans encrusted with old shit . . . careful, in letting down his trousers, not to let the cuffs fall into the urine grooves in front" (p. 123).

Midway through the novel, the man experiences the vision of cyclic continuity described to him by the teacher.

[He] walks out in the direction of the main breakwater swinging out into the ocean. The sounds of violent work grow fainter as the wind rises past him, and keeping to the edge where he can see quite far down into the sea, he walks without any hurry, not having to think about time or going back, feeling almost happy in his suspended loneliness, until he comes to a flight of stairs built into the side of the breakwater, lead- ing down into the sea. He leans over and looks at the steps. They de- scend in a simple line all the way down, dipping into the sea until they are no longer visible from above. The man sits down, and, feeling now a slight pain at the back of his neck, throws back his head. Small clouds, very white, hold themselves, very far away, against a sky that is a pale, weak blue, and when the man looks down again into the sea the water of it looks green and deep. A sea gull, flying low, makes a single hoarse noise that disappears into the afternoon, and the white bird itself flies off in the direction of the harbor and its inaudible noise, beautiful and light on its wing [p.132].

The intensity of this vision of cyclic beauty and recurrence is re- inforced by a shift to the present tense, a stylistic device that Armah uses intermittently throughout the novel to signal both immediacy and the changelessness of the ongoing cycle of natu- ral process.

In the concluding events of the novel, the man's vision is tested by his involvement with Koomson, a former schoolmate whose political corruption mirrors the filth of Takoradi. The man has reluctantly maintained a friendship with him. Over the man's objections, Koomson has convinced the man's wife and mother-in-law to record their names as the owners of a fishing boat Koomson purchased with embezzled government funds. During a military coup, the man returns home from work one day to find Koomson hiding in his bedroom, seeking his help in fleeing the country in the fishing boat. As soldiers of the new regime approach the man's house, he and Koomson run to a public latrine and lock the door. What follows is the man's immersion in the filth he has been skirting.

Koomson and the man escape through the hole of the latrine and thence through the small opening to the outside used by the night-soil man when he removes the overflowing buckets. Koomson first enters the latrine hole feet first, though the man tells him that he'll "get stuck. . . . Head first . . . is the only way." Koomson tries it head first:

> This time Koomson's body slipped through easily enough, past the shoulders and down the middle. But at the waist it was blocked by some other obstacle. The man looked at the hole again but there was space there. Perhaps the latrine man's hole outside was locked. The wooden latch securing it would be quite small, and should break with a little force.
>
> "Push," the man shouted. . . . Quietly now, he climbed onto the seat, held Koomson's legs and rammed them down. He could hear Koomson strain like a man excreting, then there was a long sound as if he were vomiting down there. But the man pushed some more, and in a moment a rush of foul air coming up told him the Partyman's head was out [pp. 196–98].

In this mock birth, the man is the symbolic midwife of his own and Koomson's regeneration into filth.

The man accompanies Koomson to the harbor where the fishing boat is waiting. He boards the boat with Koomson but jumps overboard at the edge of the harbor to swim back to shore. As he nears the beach he nearly drowns, and the description again implies a birth.

> The man let himself drop deep down into the water. He stayed there as long as he could, holding his breath. He held his breath so long that he began to enjoy the almost exploding inward feeling that he was perhaps no longer alive. But then it became impossible to hold on any longer. . . . The surface seemed so far up that he thought it would never come, but

suddenly the pressure around his neck and in his ears was no more and he opened his eyes again [p. 210].

The near-death is a chosen one, the man's ritual union with the sea and with the cyclic strength of natural process signaling a rebirth that counters the mock regeneration he has just experienced with Koomson.

The man awakens on the beach to the beauty of furling waves and a sun high in the sky, but it is clear that his own sense of spiritual renewal does not extend to the world around him: he almost immediately encounters a madwoman, a bus driver bribing a policeman, a bird that feasts on excrement, and a group of small boys "chipping away on gravestones," scavenging for marble and symbolically chipping away at the cyclic continuity with the past that the man's vision embodies. Though perhaps one of "the beautyful ones" has been born, life in Takoradi goes on as usual.

John Grimes and the man attain a vision that represents at least a limited victory over the chaos of time. But as vision is not translated into action, little or nothing is changed in the landscape of No Man's Land. Another kind of victory, still a limited one, belongs to the character in black fiction whose strength lies in action rather than in vision. Two novels in particular chronicle the heroism of the man of action—*Things Fall Apart* and *Native Son*. Achebe's Okonkwo is a leader in a traditional Ibo village, and Wright's Bigger Thomas is a twentieth-century Chicago loser; but their narrative struggles against time are strikingly similar. In both novels, time is not simply "indifferent" as it is in *Go Tell It on the Mountain*: rather, it embodies a malevolence that seems specifically directed at the two main characters. Moreover, unlike the man or John Grimes, neither Okonkwo nor Bigger has achieved any sustaining alliance with mythic time; on the contrary, their inner rhythms have gone awry and when they have been goaded into rebelling against time their rebellion takes the shape of violence, not of vision.

The narrative structure of *Things Fall Apart* is defined by Okonkwo's relationship with the earth goddess, Ani, and the ever-increasing seriousness of the offenses he commits against her. During the Week of Peace that precedes the planting of the yam crop he beats his wife, and the priest Ezeani (the priest of the goddess of the earth) explains to him the seriousness of the act:

You know as well as I that our forefathers ordained that before we plant any crops in the earth we should observe a week in which a man does not say a harsh word to his neighbor. We live in peace with our fellows to honor our great goddess of the earth without whose blessing our crops will not grow. You have committed a great evil. . . . The evil you have done can ruin the whole clan. The earth goddess whom you have insulted may refuse to give us her increase, and we shall all perish [p. 32].

Later, when his gun accidentally goes off during a funeral celebration, Okonkwo kills a clansman, again, "a crime against the earth goddess . . . and a man who committed it must flee from the land" (p. 117). At the conclusion of the novel, after his unsuccessful attempt to arouse Umuofia to battle against the British, Okonkwo hangs himself. A fellow villager explains to the District Commissioner, who has come in search of Okonkwo: "It is an abomination for a man to take his own life. It is an offense against the Earth, and man who commits it will not be buried by his clansmen. His body is evil, and only strangers may touch it" (p. 190).

The narrative is structured by three increasingly violent acts, each an offense against Umuofia and against the goddess of the earth and each jeopardizing the well-being of Umuofia. But for each, the village social and religious structure provides a clearly defined, essentially sacrificial, response. For the beating, Okonkwo must sacrifice to Ani "one she-goat, one hen, a length of cloth and a hundred cowries" (p. 32). For the killing, Okonkwo must go into exile for seven years. After his departure, his fellow villagers, as "messengers of the earth goddess," sacrifice Okonkwo's material possessions: they "set fire to his house, demolish his red walls, kill his animals and destroy his barn," thus "cleansing the land which Okonkwo had polluted with the blood of a clansman" (p. 117). After Okonkwo's suicide, his body is to be buried by strangers, and the village will "make sacrifices to cleanse the desecrated land" (p. 190).

These three offenses against the earth are public, open to the view of all, and because of the ritual actions described their potential disruption of the cyclic order of Umuofia is circumvented. Okonkwo ends as an abomination, but the village—for the meantime—has retained its spiritual integrity and strength, despite the intrusion of colonialism and Christianity. Umuofia survives, its social and spiritual structure intact, even as Okonkwo fails.

Okonkwo fails not because of his public offenses but because of an inner estrangement from time, which remains publicly unacknowledged and therefore ritually unredeemed. This estrangement is not immediately apparent. The public view of Okonkwo emphasizes his courage and his seemingly secure place in the continuity of village life. As the first paragraph of the novel indicates, his prowess in wrestling has earned him both personal respect and a village judgment that likens him to the founder of Umuofia: "The old men agreed [that Okonkwo's fight] was one of the fiercest since the founder of their town engaged a spirit of the wild for seven days and seven nights" (p. 7). This judgment exemplifies Mircea Eliade's assertion that in a traditional society, the meaning of human acts is

not connected with their crude physical datum but with their property of reproducing a primordial act, of repeating a mythical example. . . . [Such a society] acknowledges no act which has not been previously posited and lived by someone else, some other being who was not a man. What he does has been done before. His life is the ceaseless repetition of gestures initiated by others.[8]

In the public view, Okonkwo is a hero not because he is unique but because he embodies a recurrence of mythic heroism. In the public view, Okonkwo begins the novel as the archetypal Ibo hero, a role that he publicly maintains until his suicide.

But juxtaposed to the public assessment of Okonkwo is the reader's knowledge of his character. Okonkwo's "whole life" is dominated by a "fear of failure and weakness," a fear that exceeds his fear of the gods or of social sanctions. Umuofia shares the knowledge that Okonkwo's father is a wastrel, but the reader alone realizes the lengths to which Okonkwo is led by his fear of

8. Mircea Eliade, *The Myth of the Eternal Return*, pp. 5–6.

being like his father. He comes to hate everything his father loved, including "gentleness" and "idleness." Achebe is careful to point out that Umuofia does not judge a son by his father, and thus Umuofia sees only the deeds that come out of Okonkwo's fear—hard work, the amassing of material goods, prowess in wrestling and in war, and the achievement of social status. But the reader, seeing the fear, sees Okonkwo's deeds in a different light.

In his violent antagonism to all that his father represented, Okonkwo symbolically rejects the past, a rejection that shapes both his failures and his success. His conceptualization of time is dominated, and thus distorted, by his rejection. In turn this distortion of vision estranges him from the temporal equilibrium of Umuofia. Time becomes not a dimension that he inhabits, but an antagonist. His struggle against time shapes the inner narrative of the novel.

Each of his offenses against the earth proceeds from this estrangement, just as each reinforces it. The first offense is not in beating his wife but in the time he has chosen to do it, during the Week of Peace. The reader is twice told of Okonkwo's ineptitude with his gun. At the wrong moment, the gun not only fires accidentally but kills a clansman.

The seven years of exile that follow are, literally, seven years of estrangement from the passage of time in Umuofia. Okonkwo sees his exile within the perspective of cyclic recurrence: when he has expiated his crime, he will return to Umuofia and take up where he left off seven years before. In Eliade's terms, he confers a "cyclic direction upon time, annuls its irreversibility. Everything begins over again. . . . No event is irreversible and no transformation is final."[9]

His exile, however, coincides with the period when Umuofia comes into contact with the West and with a linear, historic concept of time. Okonkwo has only secondhand experience and reports of history's intrusion into Umuofia. Upon his return, his own estrangement from time has been compounded by circumstance: he fails to recognize the irreversible historicity of the

9. Ibid., p. 89.

white man's coming to Umuofia. In his view, the white man is no different from the hostile clans he has waged war against in the past—part of a pattern of cyclic recurrence. The elders of Umuofia have received gradual mithridatic doses of history and are able to accommodate it. Okonkwo's confrontation with history is fatally sudden. At the beginning of the novel he is admired for the five heads he has taken in battle. At the end, lodged in a cyclic pattern that no longer fits, he beheads the messenger of the white District Commissioner. Okonkwo would kill history.

Okonkwo's act is replete with irony. Earlier, we have seen him seeking to annul cyclic recurrence as he perceives it, repudiating the past in the fear that it will be cyclically visited upon himself. The final pages of the novel show Okonkwo estranged from both the mythic time of Umuofia and the historical time of European intrusion. His suicide denies him a proper burial, without which his spirit will be left to wander, severed from the cyclic continuum between the material and the spiritual world. But ultimately he has no place in history either, as the closing paragraph shows. The novel concludes with a shift to an inside view of the white District Commissioner musing on the book he is going to write about "the many years in which he has toiled to bring civilization to different parts of Africa":

As he walked back to the court he thought about the book. Every day brought him some new material. The story of this man who had killed a messenger and hanged himself would make interesting reading. One could almost write a whole chapter on him. Perhaps not a whole chapter but a reasonable paragraph, at any rate. There was so much else to include, and one must be firm in cutting out details. He had already chosen the title of the book, after much thought: *The Pacification of the Primitive Tribes of the Lower Niger* [p. 191].

This shift in point of view indicates the irrelevance of Okonkwo's tragedy in terms of a historical view. To the Commissioner, Okonkwo's story rapidly loses its historical significance (not to mention any mythic significance) and comes to be regarded as a mere anecdote—perhaps without any relevance to the progress of Western "civilization" in Africa. Throughout *Things Fall Apart* the narratives of public heroism and inner estrangement run parallel. At the conclusion of the novel the narratives converge, the abomination of Okonkwo's body a final true reflection of his spirit.

Okonkwo's first real test comes when "the year went mad" (p. 26). First there is an unseasonable drought, and then the rains come in force, but too late. Okonkwo survives the disaster, symbolically proving himself (as he sees it) capable of enduring a time sequence gone awry; he comforts himself in later years by remembering: "Since I survived that year, I shall survive anything" (p. 27).

An event that brings Okonkwo into direct involvement with Agbala, the Keeper of Time, assumes central importance. Ezinma, Okonkwo's eldest daughter, whom he dotes on, is an *ogbanje* child, for whom cyclic recurrence bears the notion of fatality, and her parents fear continually she will die. She has frequently been ill, but the fact that she has lived to about eleven has in part allayed her parents' fears and encouraged them to believe that the malicious *ogbanje* spirit has grown tired of the struggle and given up. When Ezinma once again becomes ill the priestess of Agbala takes her on her back and in ritual fashion runs with her to the farthest village of the clan and circles back to the sacred cave of the oracle. Ezinma's mother, watching from the darkness, can "see the hills looming in the moonlight. They formed a circular ring with a break at one point through which the foot-track led to the center of the circle. As soon as the priestess stepped into this ring of hills her voice was not only doubled in strength but was thrown back on all sides. It was indeed the shrine of a great god" (pp. 101–02). As the priestess takes Ezinma into the sacred cave at the center of the circle, she symbolically presents her to the oracle for a regeneration into the goodness of time, a renewal into life. The ritual proves successful. Ezinma lives.

This chapter has been criticized for arousing an interest in Ezinma that is left unsatisfied, since after this event the child more or less disappears from the novel.[10] Ezinma is an appeal-

10. For example, Arthur Ravenscroft, *Chinua Achebe*; and G. D. Killam, "Language and Theme in *Things Fall Apart*."

ing character, and it is disappointing to lose sight of her; but in
structural terms, she serves as an important foil to Okonkwo's
unsuccessful struggle against time. The chapter justifies itself
by showing the ritual redemption of time and demonstrating
that there are resources within Umuofia that could transmute
Okonkwo's conflict with time into an alliance with it. Juxtaposed
with Ezinma's success, after only a short intervening chapter, is
Okonkwo's accidental killing of his clansman, the impetus for his
exile and ultimately for his suicide. Ezinma is renewed by time
and Okonkwo destroyed by it because his estrangement from
time remains hidden: acknowledged, it could be healed.

The critical reception given *Native Son* bears comparison to
that accorded *Things Fall Apart* in that it has been described
more than once as having changed the course of black fiction in
the United States. But the circumstances of Bigger Thomas, its
protagonist, bear little obvious resemblance to those of Okonkwo. Born in a Chicago ghetto, poverty-stricken, Bigger shares a
one-room, rat-infested tenement apartment with his mother and
a younger sister and brother, his father having vanished long before. Achebe's intention is to repair the foundations of the past;
Wright's rage is at the inhumanity of the present.

The values of Bigger's world are implicit in the opening
passage. An alarm clock jangles, and Bigger's mother remarks,
"You going to have to learn to get up earlier than this, Bigger, to
hold a job" (p. 14). Time is equivalent to money. Mr. Dalton,
who owns the tenement in which the Thomas family lives and
who hires Bigger as a chauffeur, epitomizes the power inherent
in the ownership of both time and money. Bigger controls neither. His expected role is to march unthinkingly to the rhythm
of the novel's innumerable clocks, to accept the temporal dispossession in which he is expected to exist. Instead, through violence, he achieves at least a momentary victory over time and
thereby over his victimization. If his victory is Pyrrhic, he nevertheless bears witness to the power of a sense of time antithetical
to the secular fragmentation of the world he inhabits.

The narrative of the first two parts of the novel, "Fear" and
"Flight," is structured by Bigger's four acts of violence. In the
opening pages of the novel, Bigger kills a rat by smashing its

head with a frying pan. Later, when he meets his three friends to carry out the robbery of Blum's, he becomes angry at one of them, Gus, trips him, pins him to the floor, and threatens to decapitate him. Twelve hours after his threat to Gus, he suffocates Mary and decapitates her in order to fit her corpse into the furnace. After he and Bessie have taken refuge in a deserted, condemned tenement, he kills Bessie, hitting her head with a brick until it is a "sodden mass" (p. 224). The similarity to Okonkwo's acts of violence in *Things Fall Apart* is striking, both in the echo of Okonkwo's prowess at taking heads in war and later in rebellion against the District Commissioner and in the significance that Bigger's acts have in relation to time. Okonkwo's violence comprises an offense against the cyclic continuum of Umuofia; Bigger's represents a revolt against the linear straitjacket of Chicago. The objects of their violence differ, but both men are clearly at odds with the time of their respective worlds.

The source of Okonkwo's offense is an inner fear; Bigger's revolt feeds on an inner rhythm that defies the linearity of those around him.

These were the rhythms of his life: indifference and violence; periods of abstract brooding and periods of intense desire, moments of silence and moments of anger—like water ebbing and flowing from the tug of a far-away, invisible force. Being this way was a need of his as deep as eating. He was like a strange plant blooming in the day and wilting at night; but the sun that made it bloom and the cold darkness that made it wilt were never seen. It was his own darkness, a private and personal sun and darkness. He was bitterly proud of his swiftly changing moods and boasted when he had to suffer the results of them [p. 31].

If Bigger's inner rhythms echo the cycle of Umuofia in their imagery of sun and darkness, growth and death, they pervert the involvement and optimistic sense of community control into "indifference and violence." Bigger's isolation is equivalent to Okonkwo's, and time for Bigger too ultimately becomes lethal: the "consequences" of this inner rhythm lead to Bigger's execution. Yet unlike Okonkwo, Bigger achieves a momentary victory over time. It is this victory to which he alludes in his final "boast" to his lawyer: "When a man kills, it's for something. . . . I didn't know I was really alive until I felt things hard enough to kill for them" (p. 392). Thus, as in *Things Fall Apart*, the irony proceeds from a discrepancy between the inner and the outer, a discrepancy in which the outer esteem and inner defeat of Okonkwo are reversed in the external defeat and the (momentary) inner victory of Bigger.

Bigger experiences this sense of inner victory after each of his acts of violence; through violence he achieves a momentary control over time, imposing his own rhythm on the clocks that seek to control him. After Bigger kills the rat he dangles its corpse in front of his sister, making her faint. When she recovers, she chides Bigger, not for frightening her but for nearly causing her to be "late for her sewing class" at the YWCA. Bigger has disrupted times, and the incident foreshadows the effect of his violence throughout the narrative. He threatens to decapitate Gus in order to teach him "not to be late" (p. 41), yet Gus's assertion that he is not late, that there is still time to carry out the robbery, is confirmed by the clock. "Late" for Bigger is defined by his own inner rhythms; he imposes his definition on his friends— "Shut up! It *is* late" (p. 41)—and the robbery goes unexecuted. Here, through a second act of violence, Bigger has asserted his ownership of time and his defiance of clocks; he would make the world run according to his own inner "clock."

Bigger's suffocation of Mary ironically recapitulates the timing planned for the robbery—"between three and four o'clock when the white policeman is around the corner." Twelve hours later—by the clock— Bigger's crime is a mock repetition of the robbery: the victim is white; the crime occurs under the surveillance of a white-dialed clock, which glows and ticks in the background; and the mock policeman, Mary's blind mother, is literally unseeing. Bigger's earlier "indifference" to the robbery erupts into "violence." Throughout the description of Mary's suffocation and decapitation Bigger is intensely aware of the time shown on various clocks, culminating in an intense sense of victory over them. He checks the clock after Mary's mother has left and he has discovered Mary is dead: "five minutes past three" (p. 87); after he has cut off Mary's head in order to get her into the furnace, he checks his watch: "It was four o'clock" (p. 91). The next day, he declares that he had returned home "by two" insisting here, as earlier, on his own control of time. As he later reflects on the meaning of his crime he sees it as "an anchor weighing him safely in time" (p. 101), safely, that is, in the time of his own making. He has reduced the power of the clock to the status of servant of his own needs.

Bigger's murder of Bessie, too, recapitulates his own assertion of dominance over time. After Mary's bones have been discovered and Bigger is trying to elude the police, he and Bessie take refuge in an abandoned building. As they lie down to sleep, Bigger is sexually aroused, but his image of desire is one of time spinning out of control: "It seemed that he was on some vast turning wheel that made him want to turn faster and faster; that in turning faster he would get warmth and sleep and be rid of his intense fatigue" (p. 219). As though the act is necessary in order to master this sense of time "whirling" out of his control, he has sexual intercourse with Bessie, even though she protests. The act of sex becomes an act of violence by which he will regain control of time; and afterward, as after his previous acts of violence, it is as though he has remade time to match his own rhythms; "His breathing grew less and less heavy and rapid . . . . then so slow and steady that the consciousness of breathing left him entirely" (p. 220). As before, Bigger is momentarily at one with time, safely "anchored."

Bigger decides almost immediately that he must kill Bessie, since she knows he murdered Mary. But he can bring himself to do this only when he reiterates in his imagination the circumstances of Mary's death: "that picture . . . . of a sense of the white blur [of Mary's mother] hovering near, of Mary burning" (p. 222). If Mary's murder is a mock fulfillment of the planned robbery, Bessie's reiterates the crime against Mary. Once again, Bigger's target is the head; and once again, having thrown Bessie's body down the airshaft and believing her dead, Bigger experiences a "queer sense of power" (p. 224) that recapitulates his earlier sense of power over time, of being safely "anchored."

Bigger is ultimately caught and his power over time negated. From the beginning there is a sense that his defeat is inevitable, and this inevitability is confirmed when it becomes apparent that Bigger's successive acts of violence represent the traditional cycle gone mad, no longer nurturing but destroying. Bigger's progress from Bessie's murder to the point of his capture is one of a widening and then diminishing circle—in his own image, a turning of a wheel that grows "vast" and then is reduced to the "round flat top" of the water tank where he is finally captured, where he lies and waits as "the circling blades" of yellow light close in on him. But if the inevitability of his capture and defeat can be described in terms of permutations of the cycle, so can his successive acts of violence. It is clear that each in a sense embodies all the others: the common target (the head), the obsessive awareness of time, and the momentary victory over time unite the killing of the rat, the threat to Gus, Mary's suffocation and decapitation, and Bessie's murder. The cycle of violence accelerates as the narrative proceeds—what begins with the extermination of a rat ends with a calculated murder of a woman whose role at least is that of friend and mistress.

With each killing Bigger experiences a birth of self and of identity. But to maintain this sense of identity, the wheel of his own interior rhythms must be kept in motion, fueled by his own acts of destruction. After Bessie, who? In a sense, the only sacrificial victim who remains is Bigger himself; and the cycle fulfills itself in self-destruction. As the captive Bigger opens his eyes to the "circle of white faces," he has already been destroyed, and disappears behind the linear "curtain," "his Wall" (p. 252). The accelerating wheel has come to a stop; Bigger's later imprisonment and execution are redundant. He is already dead.

Bigger's response to timeless bankruptcy, to the imprisoning linearity of time, is to smash it and impose his own mad cyclic rhythm. Though he succeeds, his very success contains his own destruction. Bigger is another *ogbanje* child, doomed to a destructive cycle of birth and death. For Ezinma, there is the possibility of the redemption of the evil cycle into goodness. But not for Bigger. As is true of Okonkwo, Bigger's conceptualization of time estranges him not only from his community and from linear time, but from the natural cycle; Bigger's rhythms are solipsistic, a "strange plant" that blooms in his own sun and wilts in his own darkness. Wright's metaphor is confirmed in the narrative as a whole: Bigger's rhythms feed on Bigger himself and ultimately destroy him.

That Bigger's struggle is against time is manifest from the beginning of the novel, not only in his acts of violence but in the events that precede Mary's murder. Bigger's day, as he awaits his five-thirty interview with Mr. Dalton for the job as chauffeur, is segmented by the clock. He notes as he leaves his tenement he has nothing to do until the interview, and time in his mind assumes an antagonistic immediacy: to get through the day, to thread his way through time, he must have money; "if he did not get more than he had now he would not know what to do with himself for the rest of the day" (p. 17). The power of linear time rests on its relationship to money: clocks run on money, those who own money own time.

In the interview with Dalton and the events that precede and follow it, Bigger's victimization by time is intensified. He waits at the window of his room, aware that "in a hour" he must leave (p. 43). Later, he hears "a clock [boom] five times" and prepares to leave (p. 43). As Dalton questions him, he hears "a clock ticking somewhere behind him" (p. 52); and Dalton's description of the duties of a chauffeur are rigidly clock-patterned: "I leave every morning for my office at nine. It's a twenty-minute drive. You are to be back at ten and take Miss Dalton to school. At twelve . . ." and so on (p. 52). Peggy, the Daltons' cook, measures experience in the linearity of years—her twenty years with the Daltons, the former chauffeur's ten. Later, in the room the Daltons provide for Bigger, he looks at his watch repeatedly: "it was seven"; "it was ten past eight" (pp. 60–61). His awareness that his ultimate responsibility is to time is shown in his musing, as he sits in his room, that "a dollar watch was not good enough for a job like this; he would buy a gold one" (p. 61). A moment later, he goes to the kitchen for a drink of water and encounters the blind Mrs. Dalton—in silence, "save for the slow ticking of a large clock on a white wall" (p. 61). Bigger will not only "have to get up earlier" in order to survive in the world of the Daltons, he must accept the fact that his every move will be made under the surveillance and control of the clock. Momentarily, as he toys with the necessity for a better watch, he entertains the hope of such acceptance, of fitting himself into the world of linear clock time owned by the Daltons.

For Bigger, however, such acceptance is impossible, and except as he momentarily yearns for a gold watch he knows this, knows that acceptance would give his own stamp of approval to his victimization and would be tantamount to total loss of self. Bigger's estrangement from the world around him, from his family and friends as well as from the Daltons, is embodied in the violent inner conceptualization of time that runs on his own rhythms. His acquiescence to the Dalton clocks, if it were possible, would represent his own annihilation. Bigger's struggle is twofold, to negate the clock time of the Daltons and to affirm his own inner rhythms.

Ironically, Bigger's sense of control over time is counterposed to a recurrent mistiming, much as is true of Okonkwo in Achebe's novel. First, during his interview with Mr. Dalton, Mrs. Dalton enters and argues that it would be "a wise procedure to inject him into his new environment at once, so he could get the feeling of things." Mr. Dalton argues, feeling that this "injection" would be too "abrupt" (p. 48). But Mr. Dalton loses the argument over the timing of Bigger's employment and the activities that lead up to Mary's death follow from there. Second, there is the accident of the tram car schedule that prevents Jan from seeing Mary home: she herself argues that he mustn't go home with her because "the cars run only every half hour when it's late like this. . . . You'll get ill, waiting out here in the cold. Look, you take this car. I'll get home all right. It's only a block" (p. 79). From there, Mary passes out, is carried to bed by Bigger, not by Jan, and suffocated by him when her mother unexpectedly walks into the room. Ironically, with a choice of timing hanging in the balance, the two women convince the men of the alternative that creates the circumstance in which Mary's death is possible.

There are other points in the narrative where time is clearly against Bigger. Mary's mother might have left more quickly; the furnace might not have started smoking at the moment all the newsmen were present in the furnace room; Bessie could have died immediately. Time, throughout the first two parts of the novel, is Bigger's prime antagonist, and as is true of Okonkwo, Bigger is ultimately the loser.

As the third part of the novel "Fate," begins, Bigger is described as existing out of time: "There was no day for him now, and there was no night; there was but a long stretch of time, a long stretch of time that was very short; and then—the end" (p. 254). Bigger has been caught between cyclic recurrence (albeit of a perverted sort) and fragmented linearity, inhabiting neither—the No Man's Land for which his narrative has provided a name, "the ground that separate[s] the white world from the black world," a place where he feels "naked, transparent" (p. 68). Shortly before his capture, Bigger "looked at his watch and found that it had stopped running; he had forgotten to wind it" (p. 237). The clocks and measured moments of Chicago have lost all meaning to him, the cycle of his own rhythm no longer exists; and with his capture the circle closes in upon him. Time runs out for Bigger, and his temporal dispossession mimes the dispossession of all black people cut off from time, both the time of Western history and of the traditional African cycle.

Bigger retains to the end a sense of victory: "When a man kills, it's for something" (p. 392). The "something" for which he kills has been to shatter the myth of the ownership of time and, briefly at least, to set the city running in a mime of his own accelerated cyclic rhythm, eight thousand armed men running in circles, closing in on him. His power has nothing to do with clocks and little to do with money—which Bigger doesn't want enough to rob Blum's for, gives away when he has it, and on two occasions loses.

Like Okonkwo, Bigger begins and ends in isolation, lacking any sustaining vision of time. Their common rebellion against time provides the complement to vision in *The Beautyful Ones* and *Go Tell It on the Mountain*: action replaces vision, the murder of history the celebration of myth.

The common ground of Okonkwo, Bigger, John Grimes, and the man is that their struggle against time culminates in a victory that is incomplete or ephemeral, or both. Where vision is divorced from action or, conversely, where the rebellious act is a blind response to the temporal chaos of No Man's Land, the landscape itself remains unredeemed. Though vision or rebellion require heroic strength, apparent in the characters just discussed, their effect on the world in which they occur is blunted by fragmentation. Imagine, however, that the scope of vision were to include both heritage and present community, and that this vision were to be translated into action: the effect would be the imaginative re-creation of an ideal from the long-ago African past, in which political and spiritual strength were inseparable and in turn were based on a unified community. Given all this, the landscape of No Man's Land would be transformed into a world of communal celebration.

A number of black writers have attempted this imaginative recreation, beginning perhaps with W. E. B. DuBois and *The Quest of the Silver Fleece*. Zora and Bles start out with a naive belief in the power of isolated individuals: they will "love" their cotton crop into growing, in order to gain money for Zora's schooling. Quickly disillusioned when the proceeds of their hard labor are seized by the white power structure, they come to realize that strength in rebellion lies with a united community rather than with the individual. By the novel's end, given Zora and Bles's leadership, the black community has united—and has indeed been able to absorb a portion of the poor white community into their common effort. Zora herself is perhaps best understood as a forerunner of Claude McKay's Bita Plant in *Banana Bottom*, to be published some twenty years later. In contrast to the many light-skinned women characters in black fiction of the pre-Harlem Renaissance years, Zora, like Bita, is black, and is described in the opening scene of the novel as sharing Bita's love for dancing and "wondrous, savage music." She also shares with Bita a sexual history that begins against their will late in childhood: Bita is raped and Zora is compelled to "pleasure" her former master. For Zora, as for Bita, education, love, and an involvement with the black community prove redemptive of what McKay has one of his characters call being "blunted in the blood." Zora is an early example of the woman character who absorbs the tools of history and uses them in the communal celebration of black heritage.

More recently, William Melvin Kelly achieves the transformation of No Man's Land in *A Different Drummer*, in which Tucker Caliban takes an ax to the grandfather clock imported from France on the same slave ship that brought Tucker's first New World ancestor from the Guinea Coast. In this symbolic murder of history Tucker recapitulates as well the heroic resistance of his African ancestor, who escaped from the slave ship weighed down with chains and over a period of several months engineered the rebellion and escape of dozens of slaves before finally being recaptured. Thus, Tucker's act is both a murder of history and a celebration of heritage; and the effect is to inspire a mass emigration of black people from the southern state where the narrative is set, as they follow Tucker in a symbolic exodus to freedom. Vision and action combine to create a sense of black community.

Much the same is true in Ayi Kwei Armah's *Two Thousand Seasons*. The narrative outline of the novel begins on the border of the Sahara and ends in the forest regions of West Africa during the time of the slave trade. The narrative has its source in a widely held Ghanaian belief that the Akan people originated in the medieval African kingdom of Ghana on the border of the Sahara—a belief that was responsible for the country's post-independence adoption of the name Ghana. Armah portrays Akan peoples living at this original site and shows the incursion of corrupt "predator" Arabs from the north as the reason for the Akan migrations southward. The Akan arrival in the forest areas of West Africa is soon followed in the narrative by a parallel incursion of "destroyers," the Europeans who brought the slave trade.

The narrative voice is an oracular tribal "we" of a community of ancestral spirits present throughout the duration of the "two thousand seasons," embodied in the various individuals whose actions form the substance of the narrative, reconstructing the widely accepted oral history of the origins of the Akan people of present-day Ghana. Thematically, the novel confronts both shameful and heart-rending aspects of Akan history; and, as D. S. Izevbaye has pointed out, "the literary model [for *Two Thousand Seasons*] is the traditional dirge of Ghana. The function of the dirge . . . is to involve the group in the suffering of the individual, and to lessen individual grief by channelling it into collective grooves."[11] But Armah extends the model beyond grief to celebration, as a closer look at the narrative will show.

Midway through the narrative, twenty young Akan initiates split off from their parent community. Their king has succumbed to the bribery of European slave traders and has lost sight of the cyclic reciprocity of the Akan "way." In their new community, the young initiates affirm the values which their king has abnegated:

> The linking of those gone, ourselves here, those coming; our continuation, our flowing not along any meretricious channel but along the living way, the way: it is that remembrance that calls us. The eyes of seers should range far into purposes. The ears of hearers should listen far toward origins. . . . A people losing sight of origins are dead [p. xiii].

The initiates' rebellion is inspired by the remembrance of a past before the continuity of time had been fragmented by the "destroyers"; and in turn their rebellion is an attempt to restore the values of a past community.

The initiates value skill with weapons, since implicit in their restoration of the "way" is the repulsion of the destructive intruders. They learn "not to fear the power of the destroyers' weapons but to learn quickly the use of that power against the destroyers themselves" (p. 23), incorporating the weapons of history into the celebration of myth. Juma, a reformed collaborator with the white men, spends weeks teaching the twenty Akans how to load, clean, and fire their guns at various kinds of moving targets.

Their headquarters is a sacred grove some distance from their parent community, and their leader is a priest, a "fundi," named Isanusi, a man

> whose art went beyond any skill of the body, whose mastery reached the consciousness itself of our people; he whose greatest desire, whose vocation it was to keep the knowledge of our way, the way, from destruction; to bring it back to an oblivious people, all else failing, at least as re-

11. D. S. Izevbaye, "Ayi Kwei Armah and the 'I' of the Beholder," p. 232.

membrance; he whose highest hope it was to live the way as purpose, the way as the purpose of our people [p. 130].

Isanusi, their spiritual as well as political leader, fights alongside the initiates, and wrestles one opponent to death.

By the novel's end, the initiates have had increasing success at countering the European intrusion. They have occupied the slave castle and removed its guns and ammunition to strongholds in the forest. They have rescued captured slaves and invited them to join their group. They have waged a successful defensive war against their parent community when it attempts to invade their territory. Though victory is not complete, the book ends with a prophecy of bright promise, in which all the people of "the way" will come together, a "confluence of all the waters of life flowing to overwhelm the ashen desert's blight" (p. 321). In *Two Thousand Seasons*, the murder of history becomes literal, the black community an army of soldiers; and in the remembrance of the past is the promise of the future.

In John A. Williams's *Captain Blackman*, the promise is fulfilled when black soldiers take over the armed forces of the United States. Leading up to this act is an excursion through time not unlike the one narrated in *Two Thousand Seasons*, portraying the history of the black American soldier. Captain Blackman, stationed in Vietnam, combines combat duties with the teaching of black history, specifically the history of the black American soldier. After receiving a head wound, he relives in dream and hallucination the history he has taught, recapitulating the life of the black soldier from Crispus Attucks through the Korean War. He recovers from his wound and initiates and carries out a plan whereby the nuclear-armed sections of the American armed forces are infiltrated and taken over by blacks passing for white. The novel ends with the revelation of this takeover.

In the sequence of Captain Blackman's narrative, history first becomes mythic: that is the effect of the difference between teaching history and reliving it. Captain Blackman's heroism comes to represent the strength of all black soldiers and the continuity of a heritage. As his name implies, Blackman becomes a black Everyman, a celebrant of mythic strength. This sense of heritage in Blackman inspires a sense of community among contemporary black soldiers, which in turn generates the strength necessary to symbolically annihilate the oppression of history. Vision, action, and a unified community combine in the imaginative re-creation of a traditional ideal.

The novel also achieves the redemption of Ananse, who in the guise of the black soldiers passing for white becomes a guerilla soldier battling for his community. This achievement is a final index to *Captain Blackman*'s redemption of No Man's Land.

The Shapes of Chaos and Rebellion

Joseph Conrad has described the responsibility of all novelists, to make the reader "see." What is brought into view, the mode and the accuracy of the vision, and its emotional significance vary among novelists and among novels. In black fiction the focus is consistently on time, and time is dual—a character's inner vision at odds with that of his world. For Armah's man and Baldwin's John Grimes, the inner vision is nurturing in the midst of temporal chaos. For Okonkwo, the inner vision is askew in the context of a society whose view of time fosters human responsibility and a sense of order. And for Bigger Thomas, both the inner and the societal vision of time are chaotic, and in conflict. Even in *Captain Blackman*, where vision ultimately combines with action and effects change in the world, the starting point is one of duality.

The causes of this conflicting duality have been implied throughout this discussion and dealt with explicitly in Part 1. They can be summarized by referring to DuBois's concept of double-consciousness:

The Negro is a sort of seventh son, born with a veil and gifted with second sight in this American world—a world which yields him no true self-consciousness, but only lets him see himself through the revelation of the other world. It is a peculiar sensation, this double-consciousness, this sense of always looking at one's soul by the tape of a world that looks on in amused contempt and pity. One ever feels his twoness,—an American, a Negro; two souls, two thoughts, two unreconciled strivings; two warring ideals in one dark body, whose dogged strength alone keeps it from being torn asunder.

The history of the American Negro is the history of this strife,—this longing to attain self-conscious manhood, to merge his double self into a better and truer self.[12]

In the dynamics of double-consciousness, which have figured on both sides of the Atlantic, identity is in conflict because the inner reality and the view of that reality from the outside are at odds. While this may be an unfortunate fact of human life in general, its permutation for black humanity lies in what has already been discussed: the outer world (the slave master, the colonial official, the overseer, the landlord, whites in general) seeks to imprison the black individual in the void of timeless estrangement; the inner vision is seeking to combat this void, realizing that it is combat or suicide. Historically, this combat, this vision, involved the retention of aspects of African heritage, development of a sense of black community in the New World that echoed aspects of traditional Africa, and resistance of various kinds to Western attempts at dispossession.

In summarizing the fragmentation of the black experience, DuBois suggests that the ideal is to "merge his double self into a better and truer self." This is essentially a restatement of the ideal of traditional African culture, in which inner vision and outer perception were unified. The isolated individual wrestling with his God is in its pure form a product of the West, as is the concept of individual salvation. In traditional cultures, the individual must return with his vision to his human community; and that community must be convinced that this vision is an impetus for order and life rather than for chaos and destruction. For example, the opening portion of *Arrow of God* is set in a traditional society in which time remains the cycle of the seasons. The main character, Ezeulu, is a priest who functions both as the Keeper of Time and as a political leader. His spiritual vision is initially at one with both the spiritual and political welfare of his community. This is the ideal that DuBois implies—the re-

12. DuBois, pp. 214–15.

creation of a community that will allow the resolution of the duality implicit in double-consciousness. This is also the ideal of traditional African culture and the ideal toward which black fiction strives. In the novels so far discussed, perhaps only *Captain Blackman* fully realizes the ideal.

This dual focus implies certain consequences for form. While all novelists manipulate time and symbolically redeem their own mortality, differences in the manner and form of this manipulation may reflect a different orientation toward time. Even within Western white literature certain differences may be described, which are instructive in turn of the differences between this literature and black fiction.

One widely acknowledged difference between British and American fiction, for example, is the British concern with human beings as social animals versus the American concern with the metaphysical struggle of the isolated individual. Concomitantly, as Richard Chase points out in *The American Novel and Its Tradition*, when the British "novel" crossed the Atlantic it became, more often than not, the American "romance," characterized by an emphasis on timelessness in the sense of Western transcendence, rather than on the timebound movement within a realistically conceived social setting. This contrast reflects the contrasting historical reality of time in Europe and the New World; the New World, with its offer of seemingly infinite possibility, including the transcendence of time, shaped the narrative structure of American fiction. Similarly, the historical reality of black time has shaped not only the themes but also the narrative structure of black fiction.

In black fiction what predominates is the struggle between myth and history, within the context of the threat of exclusion from both. The struggle belongs to a heritage and a community that exceeds the individual. Certain differences between black and Western fiction in general can be clarified further.

1. *The celebration of cyclic time*. This is the response of Armah's man and John Grimes, as well as many other characters throughout black fiction. Western literature often presents the affirmation of cyclic time, but in the context of a cultural pref-

erence for linear, historical time. Northrop Frye suggests that all imaginative literature embodies a mythic conception of cyclic time. T. S. Eliot remarks in "Tradition and the Individual Talent" that poetry is, or at least should be, both "temporal" and "timeless," both the reflection of history and of myth. René Wellek and Austin Warren, in *Theory of Literature*, characterize the romance, but not the novel, as mythic in its concept of time. As critics since Matthew Arnold have suggested, literature fills an essentially religious vacuum. In the absence of belief in the efficacy of ritual, or even in the absence of ritual itself, the artistic regeneration of cyclic time fulfills a characteristic human need. Western literature provides an escape from the linear fragmentation of time.

To some extent, the same is true of black fiction: in celebrating an alliance with cyclic time, a character finds succor from the temporal chaos of No Man's Land. But the direction of the celebration is different for the character in black fiction: unlike his Western counterpart, his starting point is one of dispossession; he is seeking not to escape time, but to participate in it. Moreover, in celebrating cyclic time, he celebrates an aspect of black heritage that in contemporary Africa and to a lesser extent in the New World figures in the immediate cultural reality. In fiction, as in history, the celebration of heritage becomes a weapon against the threat of dispossession.

2. *The rejection of history.* In Joyce's *Portrait of the Artist as a Young Man*, Stephen Daedalus yearns to "get out of history." In black fiction, both Okonkwo and Bigger Thomas attempt to murder history. They have in common a rejection of the linear fragmentation of time, but their differences are radical. Stephen Daedalus may long to get out of history, but Bigger Thomas has never been *in* it. Stephen Daedalus may disown history, but Okonkwo can only attempt to kill it. For the character in Western fiction, the rejection of history, like the celebration of myth, implies the attempt to escape time and thereby achieve salvation. In black fiction, the rejection of history is not an escape but a confrontation, an attempt to demolish the prison itself rather than to flee it.

In contrast to Western fiction, both the celebration of myth and the rejection of history in black fiction imply that the redemption of time involves the community as well as the individual. The threat of dispossession from time is not a threat of individual damnation, but the hazard of a people. Its origin does not lie within (as angst or guilt) or above (in the hands of an angry God), but in the deliberate, concerted, and often malicious attempt of another people to remove black humanity from mythic sacred time and simultaneously to exclude them from history. Insofar as the redemption of time implies salvation, in black fiction the arena of salvation coincides with the world of human affairs. Black rebellion against dispossession, in fiction, echoes the reality of traditional Africa, in which the spiritual and the political hung inextricably together, and the salvation of one's soul becomes a political act.

If British fiction emphasizes history and man's existence as a social animal and American fiction the isolated search for one's soul, it is incumbent upon black fiction to emphasize both. This is the implication of the duality of focus in black fiction, and it is a duality that shapes the form of the black novel.

Point of view in black fiction, with few exceptions, is multiple, at least dual. The angle of vision alternates between the individual and his or her world—first the character looks at the world, then the world looks back. Implied always is a central discrepancy of vision, a narrative form that mimes the double-consciousness described by DuBois.

This duality in black fiction has sometimes been recognized, but primarily it has been seen as a flaw. The three parts of *Native Son*, for example, fall into two distinct divisions, the first two books centering on Bigger's crime and flight, Book III on his lawyer's socially oriented plea for Bigger's acquittal. Typical is Robert Bone's comment: "Book III, and therefore the novel, suffers from a major structural flaw. . . . Since Bigger is unable to bear the weight of political symbolism intended for him, Wright is forced to resort to rhetoric."[13] Similarly, the chapter

13. Bone, pp. 150–51.

on the *ogbanje* child Ezinma in *Things Fall Apart* (chapter 11) has been faulted because critics have felt the interest aroused in Ezinma should have been followed through in later chapters. What has happened in both novels is that the seams between two points of view have not been sewn smoothly enough; but these seams, which show clearly, are instructive of others sewn less obviously. Both Wright and Achebe, employing a third-person voice with selective omniscience, give now the central character's angle of vision as he views the world, then the angle of vision the world takes in viewing him. In Book III of *Native Son* and chapter 11 of *Things Fall Apart* the world looks back. A similar alternation between the inner and the outer world pervades black fiction, and is thematically essential.

In *Go Tell It on the Mountain*, this angle of vision allows the flexibility necessary to present both John Grimes's vision of his heritage and the vision which his heritage holds of him, in the persons of his mother, stepfather, and aunt. *The Beautyful Ones* begins not with the central character's vision of the world but rather with a bus conductor's view of him as a "bloodyfucking son of a bitch," and the blindness of Takoradi to his vision is an important aspect of the man's strength. Other black novelists who use the same angle of vision for much the same purpose include William Attaway, William Demby, Ernest Gaines, Cyprian Ekwensi, Kristin Hunter, Zora Neale Hurston, George Lamming, Claude McKay, Paule Marshall, Margaret Walker, John A. Williams, Alice Walker, Julian Mayfield, Wole Soyinka, and many others.

This narrative point of view allows the novelist to manipulate the reader's sense of intimacy with or distance from a character at any given time. In "Down by the Riverside," Wright at times describes what Mann, the central character, sees impersonally, in the language and diction of a fairly formal narrative voice. Elsewhere Mann's thoughts are paraphrased, still in a fairly formal manner. At still other times, the reader is allowed direct access to Mann's thoughts and his vision. In the opening paragraph of the novel these three options succeed one another, with the effect of rapidly drawing the reader into an intimate sympathy:

Each step he took made the old house creak as though the earth beneath the foundations were soggy. He wondered how long the logs
which supported the house could stand against the water. But what really worried him were the steps; they might wash away at any moment,
and then they would be trapped. He had spent all that morning trying
to make them secure with frayed rope, but he did not have much faith.
He walked to the window and the half-rotten planks sagged under his
feet. He had never realized they were that shaky. He pulled back a tat-
tered curtain, wishing the dull ache would leave his head. Ah been fe-
verish all day. Feels like Ah got the flu.

At the end of the novel, when Mann is shot, Wright reverses the
direction.

Ahll die fo they kill me! Ahll die. . . . He ran straight to the right,
through the trees, in the direction of the water. He heard a shot . . . and
then suddenly he could feel and hear no more. . . . One of the soldiers
stooped and pushed the butt of his rifle under the body and lifted it
over. It rolled heavily down the wet slope and stopped about a foot
from the water's edge; one black palm sprawled limply outward and upward, trailing in the brown current.

In the closing lines the reader sees Mann's death from the point
of view of the alien soldier; the poignancy of his death lies partly
in the discrepancy between this alienness and the intimacy the
reader has experienced in the preceding chaos of the flood.
The moment of greatest sympathy coincides with Mann's
death—and then, immediately, Mann becomes an object seen
from an alien distance. The resulting emotional shock is typical
of Wright.

Wright uses this kind of juxtaposition throughout *Native Son*.
The reader is closest to Bigger Thomas during those moments
of violence when he smothers Mary, decapitates her, and burns
her body in the furnace. Intimacy is wedded to horror. In "Big
Boy Leaves Home," the narrative voice keeps the reader at a distance while Big Boy is involved in killing a white man and flees
to the hole on the hillside to wait for dawn. There the reader is
drawn close to him, to his fear of snakes, of the dog panting at
the opening of the hole, and above all to the view he has as the
white mob lynches his friend. And juxtaposed with the reader's

intimate awareness of his view of the lynching is the alien vision of the white mob, figured in the casual remarks that Big Boy overhears, for example, about lifting the children for a better look. The duality of intimacy and the alien vision collide and the result, once again, is shock.

Achebe uses much the same alternation in *Things Fall Apart*. At the climax of Okonkwo's estrangement from Umuofia, when he returns from exile and beheads the District Commissioner's messenger, the reader is drawn once again to the inner view of his thoughts as he ponders the inaction of the crowd in response to his act. But this is the reader's final intimacy with Okonkwo. His suicide occurs offstage, described through two alien points of view, that of the villagers as they prepare to make sacrifices and that of the District Commissioner, who regards Okonkwo as a potentially interesting topic for a paragraph in his book. Like Mann in "Down by the Riverside," Okonkwo ends as an alien object, and much of the effectiveness of the conclusion lies in the discrepancy between what the reader has come to know of the inner man and how he is finally viewed by those around him.

In *Blood on the Forge*, similarly, those moments when Attaway allows an inner view of the Moss brothers assume a special significance. These moments do not come when their victimization by the mill employers is most virulent, but when each in turn seeks some form of transcendence of victimization—Melody playing his guitar, Chinatown drinking his red pop, and Big Matt holding the boulder on his outstretched arm in a self-imposed test of strength. The shadow of their victimization, however, falls on all these attempts, all of which ultimately fail; Melody injures his hand and can no longer play; Chinatown loses his sight and, no longer able to perceive color, finds nothing special about red pop; and Big Matt is killed in a riot despite his strenuous preparation for battle.

In achieving the effect of the simultaneous inner and outer view of a character, the third-person narrative voice is eminently successful. And its success identifies the essence of narrative structure in black fiction, a structure that is consistently ironic, the discrepancy between the inner and the outer continually underscored. Implied in this ironic narrative structure, of course, is an equally ironic mode of characterization. The world, the society, that the main character inhabits is obviously of central importance: and as it looks back it acts as a foil to the protagonist's character, underscoring the nature of his vision and the reader's understanding of his rebellion. When Takoradi, for example, views Armah's man as a fool and the reader understands the quality of Takoradi's blindness, the man's vision is all the more emphasized. Much the same is true throughout black fiction; the characterization of society contributes to the reader's understanding of individual character.

This aspect of duality in black fiction has been largely misunderstood. Charles Larson, for example, perceiving the importance of society in African fiction, concludes wrongly that the effect of this importance is the effacement of individuation of character: "Perhaps the most striking difference the reader of African fiction immediately notices is the often limited importance of characterization. From a Western point of view, many African novels are almost totally devoid of characterization —especially introspection and character development."[14] Larson goes on to applaud this very lack, asserting that African novels are "novels of situation" rather than "novels of character," that the community of "Umuofia, not Okonkwo, becomes the main character of *Things Fall Apart*." James Olney goes even further, insisting that "the character in African fiction *typifies* the family, the extended family, the clan, the culture; only incidentally is he himself."[15]

Such judgments fail to see the attention to the culture and the community as a means to an end, a way of achieving the dual mode of characterization that has been described. The main characters in three of Chinua Achebe's novels will illustrate the point.

In Achebe's novels the social group is very important, but the protagonist is consistently only partially *within* it. Okonkwo's an-

14. Charles Larson, *The Emergence of African Fiction*, p. 18.
15. James Olney, *Tell Me Africa*, p. 72.

guish and ultimate death come about not because he is a member of the group or typical of the group but because he is increasingly estranged from it. Obi, in *No Longer at Ease*, inhabits a social limbo, "at ease" neither in Umuofia nor in money-hungry Lagos, unable to live up to his own ideals and equally unable to conform happily to the materialistic view of those around him. Ezeulu, in *Arrow of God*, begins as the kind of character described by Larson and Olney, his vision at one with that of the community and his role to implement that vision for the benefit of the community. But he quickly becomes the prototype of the estranged intellectual as he comes to question his god, his community, the Umuoran practice of enlightened self-interest, and himself. Okonkwo ends in suicide, Obi in jail, and Ezeulu in madness. In varying ways, they lack the capacity for survival that Umuofia, Lagos, and Umuora, again in varying ways, possess. Far from typifying their societies, their fate is an index to their divergence from them.

Robert Bone exemplifies another way of misunderstanding this duality of characterization:

The color line exists not between the covers of a book but outside, in the real world. Its obliteration is a political, not a literary task. Let the Negro novelist as citizen, as political man, vent his fury and indignation through the appropriate protest organizations, but as novelist, as artists, let him pursue his vision, his power of seeing and revealing which is mankind's rarest gift.[16]

The fact is that "the color line" and its implications frame the angle of vision for one kind of view of black character. Until the color line vanishes in "the real world," at which time DuBois's double-consciousness will disappear, it will remain as an important component of the novelist's "vision, his power of seeing and revealing." When one sees American black fiction in the larger context of black fiction of Africa and the Caribbean, it becomes clear that the color line and its implied view from the white world are but one means by which the black novelist achieves this double vision that characterizes narrative structure and

16. Bone, p. 240.

characterization. In *Things Fall Apart*, the traditionally oriented community of Umuofia provides the outside view of character; in *The Beautyful Ones*, it is the newly independent African country. In Caribbean fiction, McKay's *Banana Bottom*, specifically the characterization of Bita Plant, exemplifies much the same technique. Before the reader comes to know Bita, the views that the community of Banana Bottom hold of her are given, views that center on the fact that she was raped when she was twelve years old. The European missionaries see her as "blunted in the blood." Sister Phibby, a Jamaican midwife-gossip, sees Bita's introduction to sexuality as "a good thing done early." Since the impetus of Bita's narrative, as is typical of black fiction, is toward the identification of one's place within the community these views of her are central, even though they contradict the reality of Bita as the reader comes to know her.

This mode of characterization and narrative structure figures equally when the central character of a novel is white: In Camara Laye's *The Radiance of the King*, in which the white Clarence becomes a member of a traditional West African community, the reader learns as much of Clarence through the eyes of the community as he does from his access to Clarence's inner life, and the two views are consistently at odds. At the conclusion of the novel, when Clarence has his vision of the king whom he has been longing to see, the poignantly comic upshot of this continued duality is that the reader realizes that it is no vision at all but a continuation of Clarence's illusions. What Laye achieves in this symbolically conceived novel is a narrative that juxtaposes the myth and the reality of Africa. The extent of Clarence's romantic naïveté is such that he does not realize, for example, that "the woman" who comes to his bed each night is in fact a succession of young maidens, who conceive a succession of half-white children. In order to portray Clarence's lack of vision, the view from the outside is more than incidental.

Perhaps unique in black fiction is Lamming's *Natives of My Person*, in which the large cast of characters is drawn exclusively from the white world. Nevertheless, a similar duality of vision is apparent, one that shapes both characterization and narrative structure. The novel is constructed around a sixteenth-century criss-crossing of the Atlantic in which a ship's cargo was likely to include either simultaneously or in quick succession European goods and guns, African slaves, European colonists, and Caribbean sugar. The group of "Lime Stone" (British) colonists whom Lamming distributes between two ships, the *Reconnaissance* and the *Penalty*, epitomize the European desire to scuttle the past. Each of the characters is in flight from a personal past of crime, sordid sexual liaisons, or disastrous marriage and from a corrupt world that is hypocritical, decadent, and filled with intrigue—a world epitomized in the novel by the character of Gabriel Tate de Lysle, the Lord of the House of Trade and Justice and the progenitor of sugar manufacture in England.

As he chronicles the journey of these Lime Stone colonists to "San Cristobal" (Barbados), Lamming portrays colonialism and the slave trade from the European point of view—or rather, he portrays the European point of view from that of a contemporary Caribbean writer. The characters are European; the sentiments they express are those of their historical counterparts. But the effect throughout is ironic: the European damns himself by simply being himself. *Natives of My Person* is a novel about white people in which the history of slavery and colonialism from the black viewpoint is simultaneously implied. The Lime Stone colonists' attempt to repudiate the past is defeated, as such attempts typically are throughout black fiction: symbolically, the death of the spirit that Tate de Lysle represents awaits the colonists in the New World. Like other characters in black fiction, the colonists carry their past with them, and the European journey to the New World is a return to the old.

Aboard the ironically named *Reconnaissance* are six officers and a crew that hails from various European ports. Aboard the symbolically named sister ship, the *Penalty*, are three of the ship's officers' wives, whose presence is known only to the Commandant of the *Reconnaissance*. That these women represent the past that the men seek to repudiate emerges clearly in the litany of shame and crime by which the men are linked to them. One of the officers, Boatswain, believes he has strangled the Commandant's former wife, by whom he was taken as a lover because she wanted to degrade herself. The second-in-command, Pinteados, was recruited from an insane asylum where he had sought unofficial political asylum and had a passionate affair with the wife of another of the ship's officers, Surgeon. A fifth officer, Steward, is in flight from Tate de Lysle, who successfully conspired to make Steward unknowingly have an affair with his own daughter and then revealed the relationship to him.

As the *Reconnaissance* nears San Cristobal, Steward and Surgeon learn that their wives are aboard the *Penalty*. The two officers and the Commandant learn also of their wives' various sexual liaisons with the other officers. In a melodramatically symbolic scene, the journey is capped, not by the arrival in the New World, but by death: the Commandant, Steward, and Surgeon are shot. Pinteados is left in command of a deserted ship, the crew having meanwhile set out for the island of San Cristobal in longboats. He plans to take the *Reconnaissance* on to San Cristobal, where its rightful owner, the Commandant's wife, has been set ashore by the *Penalty*, along with the other wives.

The final scene of the novel offers a conversation among the three wives—unknowingly, widows. Each in turn explains how her husband is a "native of her person." The phrase has the ring of a custom that figured among various peoples of traditional West Africa, in which the personal servants of a chief who died were expected to accompany him on his journey to the other world—to die with him. The trans-Atlantic journey has become a journey to death, a journey in which the women have led their "natives" to their doom—and to spiritual as well as physical death. The women, owners of a time that demands the sacrifice of the spirit, describe themselves as a "future" that their husbands must "learn." But the lesson, the future, that they have to offer is one of death; and, though they do not yet know it, their husbands have already learned it. The widows become powerful symbols of the way in which the New World shapes the contingencies of black time. In recapitulating in the present the spiritual death which the past implied, the women become embodiments of the *ogbanje* cycle of death: the *Reconnaissance*, led by the *Penalty*, has traveled full circle.

Lamming uses the two ships to imply the duality of the inner character and the outer world. In their journey, the men on the *Reconnaissance* had thought to find a world free of the duplicity of Lime Stone, where they could begin again, shaping their new world to fit their own vision. When they realize that Lime Stone has traveled with them, their response is horror, and ultimately death. Anchored in the Atlantic, equally unable to return or to go forward, they are imprisoned in No Man's Land. The European owners of time are themselves dispossessed, and unsustained by any vision of mythic time, they have no means by which to redeem their dispossession. The destructive effect of the middle passage on the officers of the *Reconnaissance* is total.

What Lamming achieves in *Natives of My Person* is the murder of history: the dispossession implicit in black time returns to its origins and proves lethal to those who created it. The essential duality of the novel lies in the unseen black presence whose effects resonate in the catastrophic denouement of the narrative. In *Natives of My Person*, the world that looks back is the world of black experience, and the mode of its vision is one of retribution.

A further duality, apparent in *Natives of My Person* and throughout black fiction, is that between past and present, typically portrayed through the novelist's use of memory. Memory unlocks time and allows the character himself to "see" his own duality as he becomes both the seer and the seen. If he has achieved a sustaining vision of time, as Elizabeth Grimes has in *Go Tell It on the Mountain*, his view of his own past is in turn a source of sustenance, for his vision and his past are inextricable. If he has not come to terms with time, memory may destroy him, as it seems to do in *Natives of My Person*: the officers of the *Reconnaissance* realize the immanence of the past in the present and the consequence of this vision is death. Typically, as in *Natives of My Person*, the remembered past is not only personal but the embodiment of a heritage: the characters' personal memories of Lime Stone are also the chronicles of European corruption. In *Go Tell It on the Mountain*, the combined memories of Gabriel, Florence, and Elizabeth summarize a heritage of dispossession and poverty; and when Florence in turn recalls the memories of her mother, the chronicle expands to include slavery and Reconstruction. The task of the character in black fiction is to find a unified vision that lends order to the duality of past and present, a continuity by which he may redeem himself from temporal dispossession. Insofar as his personal past also embodies the past of his heritage, the redemption extends outward to include all those who share that heritage.

In *Fragments*, *No Longer at Ease*, and *The Interpreters*, the use of memory is representative of black fiction generally. Memory juxtaposes past and present and, to varying degrees, fuses the past of personal experience with the past of a cultural heritage, underscoring the necessity of accepting, rather than attempting to escape, the past.

In *Fragments*, Juana takes a walk along the beach a mile or so west of the city of Accra, in Ghana, and sees "over in the far distance . . . the white form, very small at this distance, of the old slave castle which had become the proud seat of the new rulers, the blind children of slavery themselves" (p. 52). The castle, which Armah leaves unnamed, is Christiansborg Castle, built by the Swedes in 1569 as a fortified headquarters from which they engaged in the slave trade. When, during colonial times, the Gold Coast territorial seat was moved from Cape Coast to Accra, the British used the castle as the official residence for the colonial governor. Since independence, successive Ghanaian heads of state have lived in it. Thus, the castle itself embodies a central aspect of Ghanaian past as the point where African sellers and white buyers completed their transactions. In Juana's view, implied in the Ghanaian rulers' adoption of the castle is a similar adoption of European attitudes: immanent in present leadership is a past shame.

For Juana, as the descendant of New World slaves, the castle is the point of connection between herself and her African heritage. She recalls her youth, with its "hope of constant regeneration, the daring to reach out toward a new world. . . . The burning of old frames and the shedding of cruel blood would not be against the making of another world" (p. 53). She used to believe in the possibility of erasing the past and beginning anew; her hope in coming to Ghana was that she could accomplish this. The castle reminds her that excision of the past is only an illusion. The momentary flashback makes clear her sense of the immanence of her own past that parallels the historic immanence of the castle.

Her thoughts go back to the early days after her arrival in Ghana. She had asked a dancing partner the meaning of the Twi lyrics of the highlife song they were dancing to. His translation had been:

> Happy are those whose life is today
> and only today.
> Sad are the prophets
> and those whose eyes are open to the past.
> Blessed are they who neither see their painful yesterdays
> nor their tomorrows filled with despair:
> They shall rest in peace.   [p. 55]

The song thus reiterates the yearning of the Ghanaian world that Juana inhabits to seal off moments of time. It both asserts and denies the presence of the castle—asserts it in the awareness that the past is painful, denies it in a willful lapse into an existential present. Juana herself, in both the castle and the song, sees the desirability of denying the past for the sake of "personal peace," but she recognizes this as an impossibility, remarking to herself that such peace "would not last long." The passage is a bleak recognition of the necessity of accepting the past.

In *No Longer at Ease*, the narrator is an implied persona of the author, who not only enters into the memory of others but has his own memory. The interplay of the two becomes clear in a passage midway through the novel, which describes Obi's first day at work. It begins: "Obi's first day in the civil service was memorable, almost as memorable as his first day at the bush mission school in Umuofia nearly twenty years before. In those days white men were rare" (p. 65). There follows an account of a visit to Obi's school of Mr. Jones, a white colonial government inspector of schools, who always left his motorcycle "about half a mile away so that he could enter a school unannounced." On the occasion that has stuck in Obi's mind, Mr. Jones slapped the headmaster of the school, Mr. Nduka. Mr. Nduka, a champion wrestler, then threw Mr. Jones to the floor as teachers and pupils alike fled the school: "To throw a white man was like unmasking an ancestral spirit." At this point, the implied-author narrator comments: "That was twenty years ago. Today few white men would dream of slapping a headmaster in his school and none at all would actually do it. Which is the tragedy of men like William Green, Obi's boss" (p. 66). In Mr. Green's first insulting exchange with Obi: "Without rising from his seat or offering his hand Mr. Green muttered something to the effect that Obi would enjoy his work; one, if he wasn't bone-lazy, and two, if he was prepared to use his loaf. 'I'm assuming you have one to use,' he concluded" (p. 66).

Obi's first day in the civil service thus signals a recurrence of his first day of school, one point of connection being Obi's encounter with an overbearing white man. Just as Mr. Green's bluster embodies a now anachronistic "tragedy," Obi's cowed acceptance of it reiterates his schoolboy passivity of twenty years before. The reader has seen Obi as a person who would ideally reject the past. This brief flashback reaffirms it as an aspect of the present.

The earlier encounter at the school also embodies an implied recurrence: the unusual event of a white man being thrown to the floor gains a particular horror because it is viewed as a recurrence of a traditional taboo, the unmasking of an ancestral spirit. This linkage, in contrast to the scene involving Obi and Mr. Green, lends Mr. Nduka's blow a heroic, if fearful, dignity.

In the brief space of a paragraph, Achebe confers upon Obi's first day at work a temporal depth whose effect is one of an ineluctable continuity with the past. Moreover, in the recurrence-within-the-recurrence, something emerges about the difference between the mythic, heroic quality of a traditional African society and the pathetic anachronism of modern Lagos. Twenty years before, the past was a source of dignity. In Obi's Lagos, the past has taken on the tone of cyclic fatality: Obi, like the *ogbanje* child of *Things Fall Apart*, is caught in a cyclic evil, with little hope of renewing the goodness of time.

In *The Interpreters*, the confrontation with death is important not only thematically but structurally, as it is the repeated trigger of flashbacks. There are a number of deaths: the death of Egbo's parents, which occurs long before the novel opens; the death of Sagoe's boss, Sir Derinola; the death of an unnamed "apostle" in a spiritualist church; the death of Sekoni; and the death of Noah, a young African boy who leaps from an eighth-story balcony as he flees from Joe Golder's homosexual advances. In addition, there is the bizarre story which the albino, Lazarus, relates: "I fall dead in the streets of a strange village. The kind people bury me the following day, only, as they are lowering the coffin into the grave, I wake up and begin to knock on the lid" (p. 160). All but Sekoni's death, which has been described, occur offstage and are given to the reader filtered through the consciousness of one or another of the characters. This technique of secondhand presentation prepares one to view death not primarily as a dramatic event but as a matter of subjective and thus contingent interpretation. Bandele makes this clear when he points out that Lazarus's view of his own "resurrection" is a chosen interpretation that brings "some meaning into people's lives" (p. 179), and a variety of interpretations exists among various of the characters: Bandele is neutral; Sekoni believes that death is part of the "dome of continuity"; Kola half-heartedly acquiesces to Sekoni's view; and Egbo and Sagoe reject Sekoni's ideas. Egbo asserts that the dead are "dead," and Sagoe views Lazarus's story only as sensational material for a newspaper story, a potentially "unbeatable scoop." Major portions of the narration are given to the scoffers, Egbo and Sagoe, but, ironically, the structure of their narratives belies their own denial, affirming the continuity of time and the inextricable role of death in this continuity.

When the rain reminds Egbo of his parents' drowning, he recalls a recent visit to his home village and the site of the tragedy, then returns in memory to his childhood, to the time immediately after their death. When Sagoe awakens with a hangover in chapter 5, he remembers that Sir Derinola has died recently and that his funeral will be held that afternoon. Following this, there is an extended flashback as Sagoe remembers his first days at work for Sir Derinola's organization just after he returned from the United States. For both Egbo and Sagoe, once the process of memory has begun, it continues beyond immediately obvious associations with the dead persons. Egbo recalls his aunt, a market trader who took him for his first airplane ride, and the uncle who insisted that he bow in traditional Yoruba fashion when greeting him. Sagoe recalls his reunion with Bandele and Kola after his return from abroad and, further back, his childhood with Egbo and with the girl he is now planning to marry.

But the starting point is death. Metaphorically, death unlocks time and provides the link between the present and the past. Even as Sagoe and Egbo scoff at death as part of the "dome of continuity," the structure of their memories mimes the traditional view of the dead as emissaries from the living to those who had lived before, from the present to the past.

Moreover, death is consistently linked with water. Egbo gazes at the puddles of water forming at the edge of the roofed area of a nightclub and returns in memory to the lagoons of his village and the drowning of his parents. Sagoe's fantasy about the dead Sir Derinola, which leads to the memories that have been described, centers on the effect created by the wet and rainsoaked curtains that gather themselves about a wooden wardrobe and remind Sagoe of Sir Derinola's hat. At Lazarus's church, located on a small island in the lagoons surrounding Lagos, one church member has a vision of death walking beside Lazarus on a rainy night—in light of the imminent death of Lazarus's new apostle, Noah, a prophetic vision. After Sekoni's death, Egbo seeks consolation at his river shrine. This repeated link between death and water is suggestive of a traditional African belief:

Rain is regarded by African societies as a sacred phenomenon. We have already indicated that in some it is so intimately associated with God that the same word is used for both, or when it rains people say that "god is falling." In others, the name for God means "Rain Giver." . . . Thus, rain is seen as the eternal and mystical link between past, present and future generations. It is one of the most concrete and endless rhythms of nature; as it came, it comes and it will come.[17]

The linkage with water reinforces the regenerative quality of death as an integral part of the continuity between past and present. As an aspect of narrative technique, the triggering of memory by images of water or thoughts of death become equiv-

17. J. S. Mbiti, *African Religions and Philosophy*, p. 35.

alent affirmations of a temporal continuum. However much
Egbo and Sagoe scoff at this continuity, its affirmation is implied in the narrations they give.

Memory serves not only the continuity of personal experience
but the continuity of the culture. Implicit in this conjunction of
the personal and the cultural is an affirmation of community, at
least a tentative echo of a traditional Africa in which temporal
continuity signaled well-being for the community as well as the
individual.

Memory may of course be used to structure an entire novel:
*Invisible Man, Autobiography of an Ex-Colored Man, New Day, The
Autobiography of Miss Jane Pittman*. From the vantage point of maturity, the narrator looks back, reconstructing certain portions
of his life and typically intertwining the personal episodes with
political and social events. In *The Autobiography of Miss Jane
Pittman* and *New Day*, for example, the years of the respective
narrators' lives coincide with crucial years in the history of the
American South and Jamaica. Simply by having endured and remembered, they are forces for time's continuity, Keepers of
Time whose memories are repositories of a heritage.

In *Invisible Man*, the relationship between the narrator and the
events he narrates is more complex and more clearly signals a
disjuncture between past and present, a fragmentation of time
that must be faced, if not redeemed. The narrator of the "Pro-
logue" and the "Epilogue" has achieved a clear vision of time.
His narration of his earlier blindness is ironic—past blindness
counterpointing present vision. The duality of the novel resides
in the disjuncture between the protagonist as character and as
narrator. The progress of the narrative is toward a union between the two, as the character moves toward the achieved vision
of the narrator.

As a character, the protagonist initially resembles Bigger
Thomas. Caught in a cyclic pattern of increasing violence, he
learns that he is a prisoner of time (which is "owned" by the
Bledsoes, the Nortons, and the Brotherhood); and his breakout
from this imprisonment, like Bigger's, results in his isolation.
But his role as character is mixed with and ultimately dominated
by the vision he as narrator has achieved before he begins his

tale. The novel ends when the world of events and the world of vision have drawn together, as the protagonist descends into his underground refuge. What he sees is more important than what he does; and finally, unlike Bigger, he must be judged by the quality of his vision. The events of the narrative itself become means toward the end of achieved vision.

Autobiography of an Ex-Colored Man, published in 1912, pre-dates *Invisible Man* by forty years. The two are of a piece, however, in their common use of memory and narrative form.

The nameless main character of Johnson's novel is well liked, light-skinned enough to pass for white (which he ultimately does), and successful, the prototype of Yankee ingenuity. An accomplished pianist, he learns foreign languages with ease and ends his narrative as a financially well-off "white" man, the loving father of two beautiful children. His is a Horatio Alger success story that would bring tears to the eyes of the blind preacher in *Invisible Man*.

As in Ellison's novel, however, vision dominates accomplishment; and the narrator sees himself as a failure, not only because he has "sold his birthright for a mess of pottage" but because success as a "white" person requires only mediocrity. Not heroic enough to be black, he has to fit his color to his capacity. As a narrator he has a vision of the continuity of time, which as a character he betrays. By the end of the novel, as an ex-colored man, the ambiguities of his identity prefigure the "invisibility" of Ellison's protagonist. His outer color, which no one sees, is "black"; inwardly, in his own assessment, he is mediocre and therefore white; and this is what others see. The duality of his identity, the inner view versus the outer, is multiply ironic: he is simultaneously invisible to everyone but himself and, in his mediocrity, visible to all.

As a character, he moves from blindness to chaos to vision and simultaneously from personal concerns to a larger concern with cultural heritage, though in the end he retreats to the smaller world of family.

Initially, he is blind to his own racial identity. He begins school believing he is white and is shocked when his (New England) teacher groups him with the black students in her class. He grows up, his mother dies, he goes South to college. But, having lost his tuition money, he goes to work in a cigar factory, and later leaves the South for New York City. There, his continued blindness to his racial identity is clearly manifest in his relationship with the "Yankee millionaire" who becomes his patron and takes him to Europe as a valet-musician. The narrator describes this man as "entirely free from prejudice" (p. 473) and as treating him "as an equal, not as a servant" (p. 464). He is blind to the symbolic implications of his entry into the millionaire's employment and to the fact that the millionaire treats him like a slave.

As the millionaire's personal piano player, he is perpetually on call and must play for hours at a time:

At times I became so oppressed with fatigue that it took almost super-human effort to keep my fingers going; in fact, I believe I sometimes did so while dozing. . . . He seemed to be some grim, mute, but relent-less tyrant, possessing over me a supernatural power which he used to drive me on relentlessly to exhaustion. [p. 455]

[Later, in Europe] he fell into a habit which caused me no little annoy-ance; sometimes he would come in during the early hours of the morn-ing and, finding me in bed asleep, would wake me up and ask me to play something. [p. 465]

I was his chief means of disposing of the thing which seemed to sum up all in life that he dreaded—time. As I remember him now, I can see that time was what he was always endeavoring to escape, to bridge over, to blot out; and it is not strange that some years later he did escape it for-ever, by leaping into eternity. [p. 472]

Like the slave master, the millionaire feels he owns his servant's time. In fact he seems to have bought it as a stay against his own dread of the fragmented linearity of moments which must be continually repudiated, "blotted out." He is a double murderer: he kills his own time and that of the narrator as well.

Recalling the circumstances of the narrator's employment confirms this symbolism. The millionaire finds him in trouble with his "tribe": he has just seen a black man cut a white woman's throat and frightened of both violence to himself and implica-tion in the murder, he flees into the streets, where the million-aire finds him, agrees that he should not be "mixed up in such an affair," and whisks him off to Europe the following day. The millionaire justifies his relationship to the narrator in the same way that the slave master justified slavery: he will remove him from a benighted existence and offer him Western enlightenment. The narrator leaves, as did the slave, with no burden of personal possession except the clothes he is wearing on his back—and these the millionaire (as did the slave master) replaces with clothing modeled after his own. The journey east across the Atlantic, during which the narrator is sick the entire time, becomes an ironic reversal of the middle passage. In effect, the millionaire has sought to kill the narrator's past. Whisked from his savage tribe, dressed in the white man's clothes, taken across the ocean to a more enlightened world, the protagonist, like the slave, is cut off, except in memory, from his heritage. The duality between the character's blindness and the narrator's vision creates a counterpoint of benevolence and oppression, an effect that is an index to Johnson's achievement as a novelist.

When the protagonist is witness to a lynching, the reality of his blackness strikes him for perhaps the first time. From Europe he has gone to the American South, committed to the redemption of black heritage, which he sees as embodied in black music. He has spent several months collecting "beautiful and heart-rending" folk music that he hopes to publish; he has come to sympathize and identify with the poverty-stricken black sharecroppers and the barefooted children he has met and is on his way back North to find a publisher when the lynching occurs. His reaction is "shame at being identified with a people that could with impunity be treated worse than animals" (p. 499). For him, the lynching turns pride into shame, the heart-rending beauty of a heritage into degradation. The identity he had sought as a black redeemer symbolically hangs from a tree by the railroad depot. The disjuncture between the beauty of the music and the mutilated body shatters his commitment and his sense of black identity. Having rejected the pseudoidentity offered him by the millionaire, he is cut off as well from the cyclic continuity of black heritage. The lynched man's corpse reflects his own total dispossession from time.

The vision that he ultimately achieves is foreshadowed from

the beginning of the book in the duality between his two child-hood friends, Red-Head and Shiny. Shiny, whom he admires, is black, a heroic and brilliant idealist. Red-Head, whom he conde-scendingly helps with his homework, is white, and epitomizes mediocrity. Shiny is identified with Toussaint L'Ouverture, and is viewed by the narrator as the present embodiment of a heroic past. Red-Head's capacity and desires are more suited to his as-piration of becoming a banker, since he is "sure of getting the opportunity through certain members of his family" (p. 419). One of the "owners" of time, he is the automatic recipient of op-portunity, regardless of merit. Though both Red-Head and Shiny are the narrator's friends, his admiration for Shiny clearly foreshadows his later vision.

He yearns to follow Shiny's way himself, shown in his rejection of the millionaire's patronage and in his attempt to collect and publish black folk music. Eventually, he has realized more accu-rately the significance of the lynching—that, like John Grimes's "offscourings of the earth" and Ellison's "unhappy territory" of the past, the lynching and the dispossession it embodies are inte-gral parts of a heritage, that the beauty of the music he loves cannot be isolated from the violence that in part has shaped it; that, in sum, the music and the lynching are integral in the wholeness of time. In choosing to pass for white, he chooses ac-cording not to vision, but to expediency. His shame, then, is in his inability, through individual cowardice, to carry the burden of his vision. Instead, he becomes an Ananse figure, choosing dispossession and a full stomach because he lacks the stamina to translate his vision of time into action. Obliquely, his choice un-derscores the strength of black people, just as his betrayal ironi-cally affirms the vision of continuous time.

By the end of the novel, one duality has thus been resolved —that between the blind character and the narrator's vision. But another duality, of at least equal importance, remains— that between vision and action. Though he realizes that he has sold his birthright, there is no indication that this realiza-tion will make any outward change in his life.

Women: Chaos and Redemption

Historically, the contingencies of time and the dynamics of double-consciousness for black women have been equivalent to those for men, though certain historical differences bear discussion. In fiction, women share with men a No Man's Land of temporal chaos, in which the central need is to redeem time and thus reshape dispossession into a community and continuity of heritage. To a considerable extent, however, women in black fiction have been denied the psychological complexity of men and instead are portrayed as veering toward a number of fixed types.

Character types, of course, are as old as stories and abound throughout fiction from the folk tale onward, a part of the peculiar reality of imaginative worlds. Types assume a special significance, however, when certain patterns emerge related to who is typed and how. When a specific group is consistently reduced to a set of stereotypes, the reduction speaks as much to the writer's view of the world as it does of his fictional technique. In Western fiction women have often been so reduced, aligned along a limited spectrum from Saint to Bitch. Black fiction shares a propensity to type women characters, but the repertory comprises somewhat different roles.

In Western fiction, for example, the Virgin is a powerful symbol, embodying unity, love, heaven, and beauty. In black fiction, the Virgin is virtually absent as a type.[18] This difference, as well as others, is clarified by reference to the black woman's historical relationship to time, which has differed from that of Western women and to some extent from that of black men as well.

In traditional Africa, women were the biological embodiment of the mythic cycle, by virtue of procreation and childbirth. But they were often spiritual leaders, priestesses, as well, charged along with their male counterparts with nurturing the mythic cycle through appropriate rituals and sacrifice. As spiritual leaders their power was also political. Among the peoples of Benin and the Ashantis, women achieved a reputation as ferocious warriors. In sum, women had much the same relationship to time as men: they shared in the communal responsibility to maintain its continuity.

By contrast, the modern West often idealizes women as transcendent beings who exist beyond linear history, who symbolize the timelessness of eternity, the goal of the progress of history. Though procreation may be a part of a woman's reality, unless she has a male protector, procreation embodies an unsanctioned sexuality by which she becomes a fallen woman, fallen from transcendence, fallen into time. The relationship of Western women to time has typically been less direct than that of the traditional African woman. Male sensibility endows her with transcendence and protects her from time—but only if she accepts this mediation. The already-transcendent woman is by definition static, changeless; consequently, she is not frequently among Western fiction's most interesting women characters, though she appears quite often in one guise or another as the lady-for-whom-the-hero-kills-the-dragons. Men exist in time, in progress toward eternity; women who exist in time represent a regression, a movement backward, a fall. For a woman, regres-

18. Leo Marx, *The Machine in the Garden*, p. 347 and passim, offers a discussion of the Virgin's centrality in Western literature. The closest approximation of the Virgin in black fiction is the main character in Paule Marshall's *Brown Girl, Brownstones*, who in the course of her narrative grows from childhood to womanhood; but Marshall's character is fully drawn, her sexual innocence and initiation part of a realistically conceived novel.

sion is ironically a necessary first step to a participation in linear progress: without first falling into time, she lacks the opportunity to progress linearly. In Western literature, the most complex women characters are those who fall—who lose male mediation—and then by virtue of their own strength find their own relationships with time. Some move toward or achieve transcendence (Tess, in *Tess of the D'Urbervilles*); others achieve damnation on their own merits (Lady Macbeth).

The heroic Western woman by definition abrogates the male perception of her relationship to time; in becoming heroic, that is, seeking her own transcendence, she loses male mediation. The Ashanti female warrior experienced no such abrogation. The essential unity between the spiritual and the material in traditional West African society included the female as well as the male reality. One manifestation of this unity in traditional culture was the absence of the concept of illegitimacy, a term that belongs to the West: the child not "owned" by a father has no legitimate relationship to time or to society; he is born into a fallen state. In traditional Africa, all children were born with a "legitimate" relationship to both parents, insofar as they embodied the renewal of time and their mother possessed her own relationship to time, a relationship that did not depend on male mediation. The woman of traditional Africa had greater freedom of self in relationship to time; and because of a difference in the concept of sexuality, this relationship was not negated—as it is for Hardy's Tess—by seduction or childbirth.

In sum, the historical contingencies of black time for women are both similar to and different from those for men—similar from the perspective of a cyclic continuum; different from the perspective of Western linearity. The difference implies a potential variation on the dispossession from time as it affected women: insofar as their men were dispossessed, from the slave master's point of view they shared in this dispossession, having no male to mediate their relationship to time; and insofar as they were "fallen" (again from the slave master's point of view) the odds against their achieving transcendence by virtue of their own efforts were doubled because they were not only female but black. From the point of view of the cyclic continuum, however, neither the dispossession of their men nor a "fallen" status was relevant to their own relationship to time, a relationship that was metaphysically independent of men and that was generally only to be enhanced by childbirth.

In the contingencies that resulted from the juxtaposition of a traditional African view with that of the slave holder, one can imagine the black woman slave faced with certain contradictions in which the celebration of procreation, childbirth, and motherhood assumed an ambiguity: because of the practice of "systematic breeding"—a practice perhaps more frequent than is generally acknowledged[19]—the slave mother played a dual role. On the one hand, sexuality held its traditional value; on the other hand, it was inextricable from the slave holder's profit and material gain. Franklin points out that a twenty-year-old woman might already have had five children and that "bounties and prizes" were offered for effective breeders.[20] The slave mother knew, too, that she could at the whim of their common owner be separated from her children, an occurrence widely chronicled in both Western and black fiction since *Uncle Tom's Cabin*. That slave mothers recognized these ambiguities attached to sexuality, childbirth, and motherhood is indicated in the documentated cases of infanticide, an act that from the viewpoint of the traditional continuum would have been not only sacrilegious but incomprehensible.[21]

Though the historical contingencies of time for black women have been equivalent to those for men, in black fiction a consistent tendency has been to reduce women to the means by which a sense of temporal order, seeming or actual, is achieved; or, conversely, to the most immediate and accessible cause of time's disruption. In *The Interpreters*, Egbo would bury himself in the breasts of a woman dancer and thus "seal" himself in time. In *The Bluest Eye*, by Toni Morrison, Cholly Breedlove directs his rage against the black girl beneath him when he is interrupted by a pair of white men who shine a flashlight on his naked but-

19. John Hope Franklin, *From Slavery to Freedom*, pp. 177–78.
20. Ibid., p. 178.
21. Ibid., p. 208.

tocks and order him to "get on wid it": "He hated her. . . . He hated the one who had created the situation" (pp. 116, 118). Moreover, the same woman may be seen as both a source of order and of dispossession: in his sexual violence against Bessie, Bigger Thomas finds himself an "anchor in time"; but then he bludgeons her to prevent her from betraying him to the police and to an imprisonment of total dispossession. Egbo, Cholly Breedlove, and Bigger Thomas reduce the reality of female character to a single dimension—its capacity to help or hinder the masculine struggle against time.

Significantly, however, Soyinka, Morrison, and Wright make it clear that their characters' vision of female reality is not theirs, that the "reality" created by Egbo, Cholly, and Bigger is an illusion, one of the by-products of No Man's Land. Egbo's yearning is immediately dismissed by Sekoni, the character in *The Interpreters* who most nearly speaks in Soyinka's voice. In *The Bluest Eye*, Cholly's feelings are explained by a narrative voice: "His subconscious knew what his conscious mind did not guess—that hating [the white men] would have consumed him" (p. 118); so he hates the girl not because she has "caused" anything but because she is the only one available whom he can afford to hate. And in *Native Son*, it is clear from the beginning that Bigger's perception of time and all that relates to it is distorted by his own solipsistic rhythms. Elsewhere in black fiction, however, the distinction between the vision from within the world of the novel and that from without does not necessarily hold: the writer's vision may in fact reinforce a character's perception; and when that perception is as reductive of reality as Egbo's, Cholly Breedlove's, or Bigger's, "characterization" and "character type" become equivalent terms. For Soyinka, Morrison, and Wright, the author's vision includes an understanding of the type but exceeds its fixity; for other writers, vision may be limited solely to the type.

Thus, the examination of female character types in black fiction serves a number of ends. It clarifies one aspect of the recurrent struggle against temporal dispossession; it demonstrates a pattern in which the woman character is portrayed as an instrument in this struggle; and it underscores the achievement of certain novelists for whom the type exists as part of the reality of their male characters' perception, but who offer the type as only a partial truth.

Female types in black fiction range between the Priestess and the Mule. Chielo in *Things Fall Apart* exemplifies the spiritual power of the Priestess, a power recognized and honored by the community, sanctified by ritual and invulnerable to the whims of individual men and women. Chielo is the keeper and renewer of time, her ritual efficacy manifested in the renewal of the *ogbanje* child Ezinma into the goodness of time. The term "Mule" comes from Zora Neale Hurston's *Their Eyes Were Watching God*. Early in the novel, the central character's grand-mother tells her, "So de white man throw down de load and tell de nigger man tuh pick it up. He pick it up because he have to but he don't tote it. He hand it to his women folks. De nigger woman is de mule uh de world so fur as Ah can see" (p. 21). Given the contingencies of black time, the burden that the woman must pick up is the responsibility either to lend order to temporal chaos or to accept the responsibility for its fragmenta-tion. The woman dancer, the black girl beneath Cholly Breedlove, and Bessie are all Mules in one sense or the other. The Mule is exploited, not honored, a scapegoat rather than a redeemer, whose power over time is neither chosen nor real, but an illusion imposed upon her by another person, usually a man.

In between the Priestess and the Mule are a number of charac-ter types whose temporal power varies. The Conjure Woman's power over time is real but used primarily to benefit an individ-ual rather than the community, and consequently is ambiguous. Mammy-Wattah refuses to confine her liaisons to any one man, but the means of her power over time lies in her sexuality; per-haps as a result, she tends to become the Whore, her spiritual strength given over for the sake of material gain. The Forbidden Woman, viewed as the property of an individual man or group of men, is not in herself powerful, but she may be the catalyst for the spiritual disruption of time; her power is only seeming and only negative—she is the perceived way to No Man's Land, not to redemption. Two female types are dependent upon their re-lationship to children for a power of temporal redemption almost equal to that of the Priestess: the Woman, in her ability to bear children, and the Mother, in her capacity to nurture them, both celebrate the traditional value of children as the spiritual posterity of the community, the embodiment of a continuous heritage.

In *Fragments* the Priestess is Naana, a Keeper of Time in the twentieth-century city of Accra. Naana's stream-of-consciousness meditations on the redemption of time, which frame the novel, offer a view of time and life that recalls a traditional cyclic order: "Death, . . . now I see in it another birth, just as among you [the ancestral spirits] the birth of an infant here is mourned as the traveling of another spirit" (p. 286). But her vision, however true to tradition it may be, is impotent, no longer part of a larger communal vision in which material and spiritual welfare were inseparable. Distressed at her granddaughter's plan to hold her baby's outdooring ceremony prematurely, Naana protests: "The child is not yet with us. He is in the keeping of the spirits still, and already they are dragging him out into this world." A premature outdooring ceremony signifies a disruption of time, a disruption of the child's entry into the material world that endangers its life. Naana's attempt to maintain custom fails; the ceremony is held as the granddaughter has planned, and the baby dies. Naana's vision, though accurate, is without strength. She too soon dies in impotent isolation, a victim of the contingencies of No Man's Land. A Priestess, a type, the embodiment of an earlier way of life, she breaks perhaps because she will not bend; and the absence of ambiguity in her character functions as the measure by which Armah charts the loss of spiritual integrity in contemporary Accra.

The Conjure Woman resembles the Priestess, but her vision is less clearly related to traditional values, her power—though it may be limited—more capable of being realized in a world of contingent time. Because she has adjusted her vision to include contingency, she typically survives where Naana's integrity would be destroyed. As a character, however, she is often only sketchily drawn; though the effects of her power may be central in a given narrative, she characteristically remains a shadowy background figure. Even so, black writers portray her as someone to be respected, even feared—in contrast to her typical portrayal in Western fiction as a comic figure to be ridiculed.

In Ernest Gaines's fiction, the Conjure Woman is a benign but relatively powerless figure. The Conjure Woman consulted by Miss Pittman in her effort to avert her husband's death accurately predicts that Joe will die while attempting to break a black horse; but her vision is insufficient to forestall Joe's death. Similarly, a somewhat ambiguously drawn Conjure Woman figures as confidante to the narrator of *Of Love and Dust*, but her vision too is insufficient to combat the destructive violence of the novel. In "Long Day in November," Madame Houbigant's efficacy is somewhat greater. She is consulted by a husband who wants to get his wife back; where the preacher's advice has failed, her advice works, even though the husband has money enough for only one-third of the visionary information she has to offer.

The Conjure Woman may collaborate with evil, as she does in Hurston's *Jonah's Gourd Vine* when she advises Lucy Pearson's rival for John Pearson's affections how she may snare the preacher. The scheme works, but one result is the preacher's continuing fall toward destruction. A similar collaboration with evil operates in *Children of Sisyphus* when one of Dinah's enemies has the Conjure Woman cast a spell that will bring Dinah back to the Dungle. The spell, if not the cause of her eventual return and death, is at least prophetic.

A more complex portrayal of the Conjure Woman is given in Charles Chesnutt's *The Conjure Woman*, published as a collection in 1899 after the individual stories that it comprises appeared intermittently in *Atlantic Monthly*, beginning with the publication of "The Goophered Grapevine" in 1887. The tale-within-a-tale structure of Chesnutt's stories provides the Conjure Woman with a depth that is lacking in Gaines's, Hurston's, and Patterson's fiction.

Aunt Peggy has specific and unquestioned powers. She can "goopher" a grapevine, killing those who eat its grapes; she can turn a black man into a tree and a white man into a slave; she can fashion a child into a bird and make a normally agile house slave into a "hot-footed, light-headed" fool. She offers her services to whoever can meet her fee. The house slave is conjured because a fellow house slave wants to replace him with her lover. The grapevine is goophered for a white plantation owner who resents having slaves eat the grapes. The white man who is made a slave is a cruel slave owner who thereby learns a lesson in humanity. Like other Conjure Women, and in contrast to the Priestess, Aunt Peggy uses her powers for the individual's benefit rather than the community's—a practice whose ambiguity is underscored by the benefits derived by the white plantation owner. Moreover, she uses her power to disrupt natural process rather than maintain its continuity, thus acting as a force at one with the temporal chaos of No Man's Land, turning this chaos to her own advantage.

Aunt Peggy's complexity does not lie in her character, since in all important ways she is true to type. Rather, what sets her apart lies in the structure of the tales themselves, all of which have two first-person narrators—John, the white Northerner who has gone South to grow grapes, and Uncle Julius, formerly a slave on the plantation that John buys. Uncle Julius entertains John and his wife, Annie, with conjure stories from days gone by, and John, in turn, gives an account of the circumstances surrounding the tale. In each story, Uncle Julius wants something and uses the tale from the past to accomplish present purpose. For example, "Po' Sandy" is a tale about a slave who was turned into a tree, which in turn was sawn up and used to fashion an outbuilding. According to Uncle Julius, Sandy's ghost still haunts the building, and therefore the lumber should not be used to remodel the kitchen of the big house. John and Annie let the outbuilding stand, but discover that Uncle Julius and his friends are using it for church services: according to Uncle Julius, "Ghosts never disturb religious worship, but . . . if Sandy's spirit *should* happen to stray into meeting by mistake, no doubt the preaching would do it good" (p. 63). Because Aunt Peggy conjured Sandy, Uncle Julius gets his church—an act of conjuration in the past negates a literal dispossession in the present. Uncle Julius's aims are not always self-serving, but may serve others or the community at large. The stories celebrate the continuity of time and heritage, in which the past may not be repudiated but exerts its power in the present. With the passage of time Aunt Peggy has not only survived in memory but has grown in stature, transformed by Uncle Julius (and Charles Chesnutt) into a Priestesslike figure who counters dispossession with an insistence on the continuity of time. In this transformation, Aunt Peggy herself—whose consistent concern was her own pocketbook—has been redeemed, perhaps in spite of herself.

Nearly a century after Aunt Peggy's appearance, a Conjure Woman of equivalent complexity, Sula Peace, is offered in Toni Morrison's second novel, *Sula*. Like Aunt Peggy, Sula is the titled character, and her importance, even though she is much more vividly portrayed than Aunt Peggy, is as much in the effect she has on those around her as in her character.

Like Aunt Peggy, she is a force portrayed in the context of a community, the neighborhood of the Bottom in a small river town in Ohio, and her role as Conjure Woman is inseparable from her relationship with this community—largely a relationship of estrangement. Like Aunt Peggy, she is regarded as having the power of conjuration. She is thought, for example, to have caused a five-year-old child to break his leg and to have made an old man choke to death on a chicken bone. To protect themselves from Sula's perceived evil, people sprinkle salt on their doorsteps, lay broomsticks across their doors at night, and attempt unsuccessfully to "collect the dust from her footsteps" (p. 98). From the point of view of the Bottom, Sula is archetypally a Conjure Woman, one who uses her power only to do evil. But in Morrison's vision, as in Chesnutt's, the Conjure Woman is more complex than she appears.

The source of Sula's power lies in her acceptance of her own estrangement from time. In her own view, she has "no self to count on, . . . no center, no speck around which to grow . . . no ego" (p. 103). The Sula of today bears no relationship to, and thus no responsibility for, the Sula of yesterday: the Sula who seduces Jude Greene is not the one who yesterday was Nel Green's friend. Sula exists outside of time, one of the dispossessed of No Man's Land. Because she sees herself as having no continuity in time, she feels "no compulsion to verify herself—be consistent with herself" (p. 103); and she decides that, in the absence of such continuity, only her "mood" and "whim" make any sense (p. 104). She accepts and celebrates her own dispossession, and she is seen as shaping—conjuring—the world to match her own fragmentation: much as Aunt Peggy circumvents natural process in changing Sandy into a tree, Sula is seen causing an untimely death when old Mr. Finley chokes on a chicken bone. Sula is more fully portrayed than Aunt Peggy. In her characterization Morrison implies that the Conjure Woman's disruptive powers spring from her own estrangement from time, which she exploits and turns back against the world.

In this solipsistic quality of her inner rhythms—her whims—Sula resembles Bigger Thomas; and the resemblance is instructive of additional complexities in her role as Conjure Woman. Bigger's inner time is distorted and cut off from that of the world. When, through violence, he imposes this temporal distortion upon the world, he momentarily feels at peace because he is at one with the world—after his sexual violence against Bessie, for example, he feels "anchored in time." Similarly, Sula uses sex to anchor herself in time, sleeping freely with other women's husbands, but only once: then she "discards" them. When she makes love, she sees herself in "the center of that silence [that] was not eternity but the death of time" (p. 105). Her lovers see her tears as her "gratitude" but the experience for Sula is an impersonal one, with "a loneliness so profound that the word itself had no meaning" (p. 105). Lovemaking brings, not connection with another human being, but the celebration of an estrangement that is powerful enough to kill time. Afterward, she is impatient to be left to her own "postcoital privateness in which she met herself, and joined herself in matchless harmony" (p. 106). In killing time, Sula paradoxically removes the cause of her estrangement: like Bigger Thomas, she momentarily succeeds in matching the world to her own inner reality and briefly achieves the only peace she knows.

Thus, like Aunt Peggy, Sula conjures time—but not because others pay her to do so but because she shares with Bigger Thomas an inner need to do so. Though there is no evidence that the Bottom is correct in accusing Sula of breaking the child's leg or killing Mr. Finley, Morrison makes it clear that the case against Sula involves more than the fact that she does not wear underwear to church suppers: the accusation is more than a figment of the Bottom's collective imagination. Clearly, Sula's celebration of her own estrangement from time poses a spiritual threat to the community, and in that sense, if not in the more specific instances, Sula conjures with evil.

But Morrison's vision of the Conjure Woman includes still other complexities that suggest both a potential for good that renders Sula spiritually ambiguous and a power for evil that far exceeds the simple capacity to break a child's leg.

First, Sula is an ironic catalyst for good, as the Bottom strives to distinguish its own capacities from Sula's perceived capacity for evil. Because Sula is seen as a threat to children's well-being, even neglectful mothers become solicitous of their children's welfare. Because Sula callously puts her grandmother in a nursing home, the Bottom augments its reverence for its elder members. Because Sula seduces and then "discards" their husbands, wives take pains to please them. In sum, because the Bottom sees Sula as a "bitch," a "roach," and a "witch," kindness and love for a time flourish as never before—an irony that Morrison emphasizes by describing the Bottom's reversion to its usual state after Sula's death: children are slapped, aging parents placed in nursing homes, and husbands are "uncoddled" (p. 131).

Where she is not a catalyst for goodness Sula is a vehicle of truth, her avowed aim being "to let others become as intimate with their own selves as she was with hers" (p. 105). For example, it is more than suggested that Sula's brief liaison with Jude Greene reveals to Jude his own reality: just as he has used Nel as a Mule to anchor himself in time, so Sula in turn uses him to "kill" time. In reversing the roles, Sula shows Jude himself—a disastrous revelation that causes Jude, stripped of illusion, to leave Nel.

In sum, if Sula clearly conjures with evil, she is also a means, however ironic, toward both goodness and truth. And in the events that follow her death, there is a similarly ambiguous suggestion of her power over time. It is as though her death mythically triggers a temporal chaos that, living, she had kept at bay, a disaster that is catastrophic for the Bottom.

In the "falling away" and "dislocation" that occurs following Sula's death, the seasons go mad, much as in Achebe's *Things Fall Apart*: rain falls early in November and freezes into an ice that holds for days, and "the sun pressed against the gray sky like a worn doubloon, [as] if the world were coming to an end" (p. 130). Harvests are ruined, chickens killed, and holiday hard cider turns to ice and "split[s] the jugs, forcing the men to drink their cane liquor too soon" (p. 131). Sickness follows the untimely freeze—croup, scarlet fever, chilblains, rheumatism, pleurisy, earaches, and "a world of other ailments" (p. 131).

The climax to a season gone mad comes on National Suicide Day, January 3, the day on which the World War I veteran Shadrack, "blasted and permanently astonished by the events of 1917" (p. 6), has for twenty years ritually confronted death in a solitary, bell-clanging, dirge-singing parade through the Bottom, urging people to face death, to "kill themselves or each other" (p. 12). On the January 3 following Sula's death Shadrack is joined for the first time by the inhabitants of the Bottom—joined in celebration of the unseasonable warmth that sends the thermometer to 61 degrees and shows the grass breaking through the ice for the first time in two months. The parade ends in an ironic fulfillment of Shadrack's plea that they face death, ends at the river where an unfinished tunnel on which no black man had been allowed to work becomes the focus of years of rage: "Old and young, women and children, lame and hearty, they killed, as best they could, the tunnel they were forbidden to build" (p. 138). But the tunnel gives way, and they find themselves "in a chamber of water, deprived of the sun that had brought them there" (p. 139).

Earlier, the death of Sula Peace has been described as "the best news folks . . . had had since the [false] promise of work at the tunnel" (p. 129), and those who had attended her burial did so not to mourn but to bear witness to the interment of a witch. Like the false news of work on the tunnel, however, the news of Sula's death is also false: the song sung at her burial had been

"Shall We Gather at the River" and in the disaster of National Suicide Day the hymn becomes in retrospect unwittingly prophetic. The suggestion is that, from the grave, Sula has the final word.

Like Aunt Peggy, Sula has a power that, it is suggested, continues after she dies, in a symbolic affirmation of the continuity of past and present. In Sula's narrative this continuity stands in a seemingly ironic contradiction to the temporal estrangement she embodied while she lived. More profoundly, however, it is a continuity that signals not the goodness of time but the evil *ogbanje* cycle, time gone awry, the seasons gone mad, in a chaotic mime of Sula's own dispossession. For both Chesnutt and Morrison, the Conjure Woman assumes a complexity that transcends not only the comic stereotype of Western fiction but the limited stature the type is granted in novels by other black writers. Moreover, the kinship between the two writers comes despite their near-century separation in time, and the equivalent separation between the antebellum Aunt Peggy and her Ohio counterpart of the 1920s and 1930s. Perhaps fittingly, the kinship between Aunt Peggy and Sula Peace manifests as well the continuity apparent in black fiction.

Mammy-Wattah is a folk figure of contemporary West Africa, portrayed, for example, in a highlife song popular in the late sixties:

> If you see Mammy-Wattah, oh—
> If you see Mammy-Wattah, oh
> Never, never you run away.

A mermaid figure, she may literally charm a man who sees her only once into never leaving her. She is a Lorelei or a Siren, but unlike these Western counterparts, she fulfills her promise, leading men not to destruction but to redemption into the continuity of flesh and spirit, a fulfillment perhaps implicit in her link with water. Like the Conjure Woman, she offers this redemption to individuals rather than to the community, but her clientele is limited to men and (unless her stature is diminished to that of the Whore) her price is not material but psychological —nothing less than a man's loss of all independence of being. In her most benign aspect, she represents sexual union with the spiritual force of the universe; but, like the Conjure Woman, she is to some extent spiritually ambiguous: like Sula, she may make men into the counterpart of the female Mule.

Simi, Egbo's mistress in *The Interpreters*, is explicitly identified as "an incarnation of Mammy-Wattah." An older woman with many lovers, she tenderly relieves Egbo of his virginity, a ritual through which Egbo achieves both sexual fulfillment and spiritual rebirth. The relationship endures for years and when Egbo later is attracted to a young woman his own age, his task is to break off with Simi—which by the novel's end he has been unable to do.

Superficially, Simi resembles the Western Fallen Woman with a Heart of Gold, but she is neither so sentimentalized nor so trivial. She does not fall in love with Egbo, nor does she discontinue her other affairs: Mammy-Wattah's alliance is not to be confined to any one man. Moreover, far from being a Fallen Woman, she embodies total spiritual integrity, and this is the source of her attraction.

Hannah Peace, Sula's mother in Morrison's *Sula*, is a Mammy-Wattah figure. After her husband's death, she has "a steady sequence of lovers" (p. 36), each of whom is made to feel "complete and wonderful . . . in the Hannah-light that shone on him simply because he was" (p. 37). Like Simi, she is held in high regard by her lovers, who see her as kind, generous, extraordinarily beautiful, and elegant—and above all as someone to be defended from gossip of any kind. Unlike Sula, Hannah never "discards" one lover for the next; also unlike Sula, her goal is not to counteract her own dispossession from time. Rather, her "Hannah-light" offers to her lovers a temporal peace that is the antithesis of Sula's offering.

As a folk figure, Mammy-Wattah is immortal and thus invulnerable to time. Though Simi's agelessness in *The Interpreters* mimes this folk quality, other Mammy-Wattah figures are themselves fragile and subject to the contingencies of time. Hannah learns that her mother has killed her heroin-addicted brother by setting him afire, dreams that she herself will be married in a red dress, and the next day dies in the flames of the backyard fire that she is using to can tomatoes. The color red indicates death; in the context of the mythic reality that Hannah embodies, Hannah is consumed by her own "light," her death a voluntary sacrifice, a symbolic marriage in which she seeks the redemption of her brother by means of the only union available to her—the ultimate offering of her body in a sacrifice that would maintain the sacred continuum of time. The ephemeral rather than the immortal characterizes Hannah, and this departure from the folk figure underscores the capacity of Morrison's vision to subsume the type in the acknowledgment of the contingencies of black time.

Jean Toomer offers an ephemeral Mammy-Wattah figure in Karintha, the title character in the story that opens *Cane*. Karintha has skin "like dusk on the eastern horizon." At twelve, she is a "wild flash that told other folks just what it was to live. At sunset, when there was no wind, and the pine-smoke from over by the sawmill hugged the earth and you couldn't see more than a few feet in front, her sudden darting past you was a bit of vivid color, like a black that flashes in light" (p. 1). Like Simi, Karintha offers to "many men" sexual and spiritual fulfillment; but she shares with Hannah an imagery of light, in which she is shown to be as ephemeral as the sunset or a flash of flame in growing darkness. In her brief narrative, she becomes pregnant, gives birth to her child on a bed of pine needles, then buries it in a pile of sawdust. In a world of contingent time, Toomer's Mammy-Wattah is no longer immortal and, no longer invulnerable to time, is in fact caught up in a temporal acceleration much like that symbolized by the old manchild in *The Beautyful Ones*.

Though the folk figure is not a Whore, Mammy-Wattah in the world of contingent time may become one, as Toomer's Karintha does. As a Whore, she exhibits her spiritual loss in a quest for material gain from her relationship with men. The title character of Cyprian Ekwensi's *Jagua Nana*, for example, a strong, practical-minded woman, is a Whore: more than one of her clients becomes her ardent suitor, at great expense to himself and to the profit of Jagua Nana.

A Whore may still be all things to all men, but only as she can foster the illusion of Mammy-Wattah's spiritual strength. Anna, in *Blood on the Forge*, hovers somewhere in between Mammy-Wattah and the Whore. At the center of the narrative, Anna for a brief moment becomes Mammy-Wattah for Melody, though her own self-image does not match his vision. Looking at Anna as she impatiently waits for him to "make love," Melody

saw her as though she had a new face. His hand came back and ran over the guitar. He didn't exactly hear what kind of music he was making but he knew what passed in his head. This girl had more than one woman shackled in her eyes. All the women he had seen were there. Here was the fat-cheeked black girl he had seen walking in the rain, the woman whose left breast died and rotted until she stank so no man would buy her for a dime. Here, quivering above the high weeds, were the freckled legs of the bohunk being covered by her brother. Here were women smelling of rut and sweat and some of milkweed crushed in the field ground under their raw buttocks, the blues singer in a Kentucky jook joint, lifting her skirt to cover coins on table corners, spreading herself before the boys, crying: "Throw your quarters! Throw a bull's eye and git it free!" Here were the women seen through a window or behind a door . . . again the sick eyes of that fat-cheeked girl walking in the rain—dead swimming fish eyes telling a lie. . . . Come lay your floating head on a beautiful-as-fresh-split-cedar belly and let your toes tickle the stars. . . . [pp. 87–88; ellipsis in original].

Anna's promise, Melody knows, is a lie, yet he is drawn by it, "the beautiful-as-fresh-split-cedar belly." Anna is all women and if all women are whores, Melody's vision of her nevertheless portrays a power that transcends the individual and echoes the Mammy-Wattah's universal appeal. And lie or not, after they have made love on a later occasion, "without trying, he had built a song around a tan-skinned girl, the shadow of her legs making a pattern on the floor as she turned down the kerosene lamp" (p. 146). Anna is a Whore, but in Melody's vision and in the music of his guitar she momentarily becomes Mammy-Wattah.

As a Whore, Anna symbolically subsumes the world of the novel. The mill workers are whores, selling their bodies to the mill owners: Melody a finger, his brother Chinatown his eyes, and Bo and Zanski (two other workers, one Slav, one black) their legs. If the mothers in this world are not whores, they raise whores: Zanski's Rosa is a whore, and the three episodes in which children figure all involve copulation, including one episode in which a line of boys wait for a "turn" at "ol' Betty," a ten-year-old girl. The reality of the Whore, rather than the illusion of Mammy-Wattah, is malignantly all-consuming of human life, and is the symbolic center of the novel.

Much as the Conjure Woman only approximates the Priestess, Anna only approximates Mammy-Wattah. In No Man's Land the Whore—like the Conjure Woman, unlike Mammy-Wattah or the Priestess—survives, a capacity she shares with Ananse, a capacity that is purchased at considerable spiritual expense.

In contrast to Mammy-Wattah or even the Whore, the Forbidden Woman has no identity independent from her relationship to men. She lacks the spiritual stature of Mammy-Wattah and even the capacity to exchange that stature for survival. Most often, she is simply a Mule—but one who cannot offer even the illusion of time's redemption, but only bear responsibility for its disruption. Typically, she is a rather wooden figure whose function is to contribute to the downfall of the male hero or, alternatively, to show his need for redemption. Clara, in *No Longer at Ease*, is a Forbidden Woman: as an *osu* (descendant of a slave caste) she is forbidden to Obi. Obi winds up sentenced to a jail term for accepting bribes and is the object of almost universal scorn; part of the scorn, though Clara is portrayed sympathetically, stems from his relationship with her. Odili Samson, in *A Man of the People*, dallies with the white wife of a European official and later woos the intended wife of a political rival. Catherine, in *Catherine Carmier*, is forbidden to Jackson by virtue of a long-standing estrangement between their two families.

Often, the Forbidden Woman is forbidden by reason of the color of her skin. Mary, in *Native Son*, the archetypal Forbidden White Woman, is the cause of Bigger's ultimate destruction, though his crime against his black mistress Bessie is both premeditated and more brutal. The Creole schoolteacher is forbidden to "the master's son" in *Miss Pittman*; because he cannot deny his love for her or face the living consequences of it, he commits suicide. Louisa, in Toomer's "Blood-Burning Moon," is a more complex example. Black, she becomes for both the white Bob Stone and the black Tom Burwell a Forbidden Woman: Stone must sneak to the quarters to see her because he feels shame at the relationship, and to Burwell she is forbidden because of her status as Stone's woman. Because Burwell does not "honor" this status and instead fights with Stone, he is lynched; and Louisa ends the story half-crazed, not hearing Burwell's final death-cry and believing if she sings, "perhaps he will come back" (p. 35). Often, the Forbidden Woman is herself destroyed, as Becky is in Toomer's story of that title: the white mother of two black sons, she dies when her house crumbles in on top of her. Clara, in *No Longer at Ease*, suffers a long illness after having an abortion. The white girl from Georgia in *Another Country* goes insane after her affair with Rufus and his suicide.

In sum, the Forbidden Woman exemplifies the extremity of female reduction and impotence. She is as unambiguous as the archetypal Priestess, though in the direction of destruction rather than redemption. She is perhaps most interesting by reason of what she is not. First, in contrast to Western fiction, the Forbidden Woman in black fiction is never forbidden by reason of her virginity. For the most part in black fiction, sexual initiation takes place before the story proper begins and the conflict, which might otherwise center on the retention or loss of virginity, focuses instead on procreation, childbirth, or marriage. Not only is she never a Virgin, neither is she ever a Rebel against her status as a Mule. She plays her part as a catalyst for destruction and either disappears or is herself destroyed. In her passivity, she contrasts with the Woman and the Mother, who potentially at least share the Mule-like status of the Forbidden Woman but who sometimes rebel against this status and assert their right to ambiguity or even independence.

The Woman, by virtue of childbirth and pregnancy, embodies the celebration of cyclic time. As a type she is simply a Woman: characterization centers on biology, but biology has a spiritual dimension, much as in traditional Africa. Mothersill's pregnant wife in *Mothersill and the Foxes* is a Woman, her significance as mythic celebrant emphasized by the aberrant sexuality and sterility of the other women in the novel. Gabriel Grimes's first wife in *Go Tell It on the Mountain* is not a Woman; and her barrenness symbolizes her dispossession from cyclic time. In the same novel Florence's barrenness underscores her status as an inhabitant of No Man's Land. Elizabeth is a Woman, and much of the novel's interest lies in the conflict between the Woman and Gabriel's Westernized view, in which she is a Fallen Woman. In refusing this designation, in refusing to repent of giving birth to an illegitimate child, Elizabeth rebels against history by remaining true to a mythic type.

In Tish and Fonny in *If Beale Street Could Talk*, Baldwin develops more fully, with some important variations, the story of Elizabeth and Ronny. Tish, like Elizabeth, is pregnant; and Fonny, the child's father, to whom she is not married, has been unjustly imprisoned. Tish's story, which she narrates herself, continues Elizabeth's circumstance and vision; but the vision has broadened in scope, embracing everyone she loves in what amounts to direct combat with the white world. Thus, vision in *Beale Street* is neither as isolated nor as passive as it is in Baldwin's first novel; and these differences spring from the fact that Elizabeth's mythic vision of time has, in the character of Tish, moved to center stage as the controlling element of narrative form and theme.

While Elizabeth celebrates her son's birth alone after Ronny's death, both Tish's celebration and her vision of time's continuity are inseparable from her sense of family. Fonny is still alive, though imprisoned, and unlike Ronny knows of her pregnancy and shares her sense of celebration, as do her own family and Fonny's father. The quality of her vision of time is portrayed as she listens with her family to Ray Charles:

I listened to the music and the sounds from the streets and Daddy's hand rested lightly on my hair. And everything seemed connected—the street sounds and Ray's voice and his piano and my Daddy's hand and my sister's silhouette and the sounds and the lights coming from the kitchen. It was as though we were a picture, trapped in time: this had been happening for hundreds of years, people sitting in a room, waiting for dinner and listening to the blues. And it was as though, out of these elements, this patience, my Daddy's touch, the sounds of my mother in the kitchen, the movement of Ernestine's head as she lit a cigarette, the movement of her hand as she dropped the match into the ashtray, the blurred human voices rising from the street, out of this rage and a steady somehow triumphant sorrow, my baby was slowly being formed. [p. 41]

Like the central characters in *Invisible Man* and *Autobiography of an Ex-Colored Man*, Tish finds in black music the continuity of a heritage—a theme Baldwin also develops in "Sonny's Blues." The moment becomes all moments, all time, the unborn baby part of a family whose heritage is spiritual triumph in the midst of despair. Moreover, because Tish and her family are united, the efficacy of her vision goes beyond Elizabeth's endurance and acceptance to include combat as well.

Her own family unites with Fonny's father to rectify the injustice done to Fonny, who has been convicted of rape. They scrape together enough money to hire a good lawyer and, after Fonny's conviction, to seek out evidence for a new trial. Tish's mother flies to Puerto Rico to find the woman who has accused Fonny and plead with her to rectify her mistake. The attempt fails, and by the end of the novel Fonny is still in jail and his father has killed himself. Even so, Tish and her family remain determined that Fonny will be exonerated, and in the child's birth there is an implicit promise of life and renewal. The family has discovered the strength of their own heritage and has put this strength to work in their attempt to free Fonny and, by implication, all wrongfully imprisoned black men.

In *Beale Street*, Gabriel Grimes's condemnatory voice and Florence's repudiation of blackness have been given to Fonny's mother. When told of Tish's pregnancy, she prophesies that "the Holy Ghost will cause that child to shrivel in your womb" (p. 68). She has embraced the values of the white world: yearning to be white herself, she fills her light-skinned daughters with empty pretensions and rejects her son Fonny partly because he is "too dark." Baldwin has shifted the conflict from the pseudofather and son (Gabriel and John) to the pseudomother and daughter (Fonny's mother and Tish). Baldwin's shift to a female central character is accompanied by a similar shift in two other important characters: though both his father and Tish's play important roles, Fonny's fate has been and will be in large part determined by women—his mother, his "victim," and the mother of his unborn child.

Because of this shift, moreover, the structure of narrative conflict becomes mythic, life versus the denial of life. The curse that Fonny's mother places on the unborn child falls instead on her husband, who commits suicide just prior to the baby's birth. And the woman who has falsely accused Fonny suffers a harsh, mythic justice: carried in agony to a hospital, she suffers a miscarriage, her own womb having "shriveled." But the novel ends with a birth and a baby crying loud enough to "wake the dead." Life has for the moment triumphed.

In sum, *Beale Street* strengthens the thematic celebration of mythic time that figures in *Go Tell It on the Mountain*; and mythic form shapes the conflict and the resolution of the narrative.

In *Beale Street* vision is put to work within the larger world, the world of airplanes, law courts, and money. Mythic vision gains power in the world of linear time. Though victory in the terms of history is still out of reach when the novel ends, the vision itself not only remains intact but has been strengthened in the struggle. Tish's admittedly limited achievement is more accurately valued, however, when she is contrasted with male characters who have attempted to combat history—Okonkwo and Bigger Thomas, for example, both archetypally masculine and both physically and spiritually destroyed in the struggle.

In complexity of characterization, however, Tish suffers by comparison to either Okonkwo or Bigger Thomas, in both of whom the ironic discrepancy between the inner person and the view taken of him is central to character and to narrative structure. If this irony exists in *Beale Street*, it belongs to Fonny—viewed by the white world as a criminal, he is in reality an innocent victim; accused of rape, he is falsely charged with sullying the mythic values that, through Tish's pregnancy, he celebrates. Tish's strength, however, lies in her adherence to her status as a Woman, a status that the novel's world is almost unanimous in acknowledging; and clearly the vision from the world of *Beale Street* represents Baldwin's own.

In short, Tish is portrayed as the ideal instrument through which all black men may be freed from the imprisonment of time and allowed to celebrate a heritage. The ideal Woman, she is given as foils two non-Woman figures—the hysterical "rape victim," and the woman who would sacrifice her spiritual posterity to fit the values of the white world. Baldwin implies that if the black community offered the world at large a description of its women, the portrait would would consist mainly of two types—the Woman (Tish) and the non-Woman (the Puerto Rican woman and Fonny's mother). This binary portraiture ignores the contingencies suggested by history and by other black writers' portrayal of women, especially perhaps those drawn by women writers. Baldwin is not alone in his typology, however: in both McKay's and Gaines's fiction, women characters much like Tish are offered as the ones who will resolve the dualities of time for all black men.

In *Banana Bottom* the female instrument is Bita Plant, a Jamaican who is able to retain her status as a Woman despite the many destructive alternatives offered her—a life dominated by the Puritan mores of her missionary benefactors; a liaison with Hopping Dick, who lives life for its pleasures; or marriage to the sexually repressed Harold Newton Day, whose "defilement" of a nanny goat is luckily discovered before his wedding to Bita. Because Bita does not fall victim to these alternatives, she is able to symbolize a heritage that in its essentials remains unchanged despite the threat implied by history. Like Tish, Bita can absorb the tools of history into the goodness of time: as the novel closes, she has married a farmer, and the reader leaves her reading Shakespeare while nursing a baby.

The contingencies of black time and the ambiguities of womanhood play no part in McKay's portrayal of Bita. Clearly, he sees Bita as she sees herself and as the world of Banana Bottom comes to see her—as a Woman whose strength lies in her adherence to type.

That this strength is a female prerogative for McKay is demonstrated by his earlier novels, *Home to Harlem* and *Banjo*, whose male characters are limited in ways that Bita is not. In *Home to Harlem*, reading Shakespeare belongs to Ray, a suffering intellectual who finds himself in No Man's Land wherever he goes, an inhabitant of what he terms "the vast international cemetery of this century." For him, unlike Bita, Western culture coincides with the death of the spirit. On the other hand, there is Jake—the Hopping Dick of *Home to Harlem*—who finds happiness with the symbolically named Felice, a Harlem prostitute through whom he refutes the "cemetery." In *Banjo*, Ray travels to Europe and finds some promise of spiritual rebirth in the world offered by Banjo, a black jazz musician. Banjo celebrates a heritage in music, but his celebration is more fragile than Bita's: he scorns the culture that Bita is able to absorb without threat, seeing Western civilization as essentially "machine-made." As Ray joins Banjo's world, he hopes to "hang on to his intellectual acquirements," but there is no assurance that he will be able to do so.

If either Jake or Ray resolves the dualities of No Man's Land, the resolution is both more tentative and less direct than it is for Bita. Ray may have to scuttle Shakespeare, and Jake's sense of a "home" is dependent on a woman. *Banana Bottom* offers a keener sense of mythic celebration; but the price is that, however delightful Bita may be as a character, her characterization is limited to the Woman as mythic celebrant. The interest of the novel lies in the confrontation between this type and the external hazards of her world.

Where the Woman is defined by her ability to bear children, the Mother is defined by her independence, chosen or imposed, from any individual man and her relationship to her children. In this independence, she is in contrast to her Western counterpart, who tends to become "the Angel in the House" (Esther Summerson in *Bleak House*, for example), or perhaps the Harried Housewife à la Erma Bombeck and numerous fictional examples. Typically, the Mother is nobody's wife; if she is angelic, she tends more toward an avenging Gabriel than a rosy-cheeked cherub.

She is often poor and raising her children alone, their father somewhere "beyond memory," as the narrator of Lamming's *In the Castle of My Skin* remarks. She is Bigger Thomas's mother in *Native Son* and the seamstress-mother of Johnson's protagonist in *Autobiography of an Ex-Colored Man*. Grandmothers, aunts, and barren women may become the Mother in their caretaking relationship to the children in a novel. At the end of *Go Tell It on the Mountain*, Aunt Florence becomes a Mother in her final confrontation with Gabriel over the necessity to accept Johnny, and this new status is an aspect of her redemption into time. Mary, the down-home landlady to the protagonist of *Invisible Man*, is a

Mother figure, and the protagonist's rejection of her for the Brotherhood is an aspect of his blindness. *Song of Solomon*'s Pilate Dead, refusing to marry her daughter's father, exemplifies the Mother's independence, just as *Sula*'s Nel Greene exemplifies her strength. In these two novels by Morrison, as in Gayl Jones's *Corregidora*, multiple generations of women share a husbandless, fatherless household.

In *The Autobiography of Miss Jane Pittman*, Ernest Gaines uses the Mother much as Baldwin and McKay use the Woman—to resolve dualities that in previous novels remain unresolved, a resolution that is gained at the price of certain complexities of characterization. In the opening section, Big Laura exemplifies the heroic strength that the Mother may achieve: baby in her arms, she leads the newly freed slaves through the swamps and dies defending them against the "Secesh." Miss Pittman herself embodies this same strength throughout the 110 years of her life. Though she is barren, much of her life is devoted to motherhood, first to Big Laura's orphaned son Ned and much later to Jimmy, the young civil-rights worker who is killed at the end of the novel. Miss Pittman's role as Mother is strengthened by the absence of biological motherhood: motherhood becomes a chosen role, her care of the younger generation a mythically conceived celebration of the continuity of a people.

In the character of Miss Pittman, the potential of the Mother for resolving another duality of black fiction is apparent. In contrast to Gaines's two earlier novels, *Catherine Carmier* and *Of Love and Dust*, *The Autobiography of Miss Jane Pittman* portrays the unification rather than the division of the black community, largely as a result of Miss Pittman's role as the Mother of generations. Her narrative recounts the progress toward civil rights since slavery, chronicling the violence, degradation, and spiritual humiliation she has suffered through emancipation, reconstruction, and the first six decades of the twentieth century. Her survival under such conditions in itself testifies to her strength, but her narrative is a testament to her vision as well. Thus, her participation in the civil-rights demonstration that concludes the novel does not transcend the suffering of the past so much as it sanctifies it and the suffering of all black people. The demon-

stration becomes a product not just of the times but of a courageous heritage, at one with a courageous life that embodies that
heritage. In Miss Pittman, history becomes mythic, and her vision unites a people.

By contrast, *Catherine Carmier* pits the younger generation
against the elder; and though the young people, in the characters of Catherine and Jackson, attempt to rebel against the demands of their elders, by the novel's end they have sacrificed
their own dreams as they wait for Catherine's father to die.
Moreover, their two families have not spoken for two decades;
this division, too, which Catherine and Jackson's marriage would
have bridged, still stands at the conclusion of the novel. In *Of
Love and Dust*, black alliances with the white world divide the
black community and ultimately prove destructive. Pauline is the
black mistress of Bonbon, the Cajun overseer of the farm where
Marcus has been put to work while awaiting trial for murder.
Angry with Bonbon, who in Marcus's view personifies the white
oppressor, Marcus first attempts to seduce Pauline; failing
there, he succeeds with Bonbon's white wife, Louise, who in turn
is retaliating against her husband's infidelity. Ironically, both
Pauline and Marcus come to love their white lovers, but ultimately the symbolic dust of Gaines's title wins a clear victory over
love: Marcus dies, shot by Bonbon, and Louise ends in an insane
asylum.

In both of Gaines's earlier novels, then, the community is divided, and each narrative ends in despair and destruction. In
Miss Pittman, by contrast, unity effaces conflict as the militant
ideals of the young are embodied in the courage and wisdom of
the old, as the heroic Miss Pittman inspires a community to action. By choosing a woman, a symbolic Mother, as his main character, Gaines achieves the resolution of a duality that figures in
his earlier fiction.

Miss Pittman's strength of character comes at a certain loss,
the measure of which is perhaps best clarified when she and the
Women in Baldwin's and McKay's fiction are compared to the
women in two recent novels written by women, *Corregidora* by
Gayl Jones and *Meridian* by Alice Walker. In these books complexity of character precludes the type and lends to celebration

an unflinching willingness to face the contingencies of black time, not only in the world but in the female self.

Corregidora provides a clear account of the ambiguities of childbirth under slavery and provides as well a vision in which the traditional African celebration of childbirth is joined to a New World rebellion against history. Ursa Corregidora, the singer whose life the novel portrays, is the fourth-generation descendant of a Brazilian slave and a Portuguese plantation owner. She has grown up in the American South in a household shared with her mother, her grandmother, and her great-grandmother. They pass on to Ursa their common fund of memories, extending back to the sexual abuse suffered by her great-grandmother and grandmother under slavery in Brazil. Corregidora, the great-grandmother's owner, had fathered Ursa's grandmother and later hired both women out as prostitutes (to white men only). Ursa's mother was the product of incest between Corregidora and his own daughter. Corregidora's sexual abuse of his female slaves makes a mockery of the traditional African point of view in which sexuality and childbirth were seen as inseparable and as sacred. Yet in the great-grandmother's vision "making generations" is nevertheless celebrated because, as in traditional Africa, descendants ensure a continuity of time. Ursa's great-grandmother wants this continuity so that the white slave owner may not repudiate his own past. She tells Ursa, "When they did away with slavery down there [Brazil] they burned all the slavery papers so it would be like they never had it" (p. 8). "Making generations" is part of her plan to make this burning of records futile. Ursa says:

"My great-grandmama told my grandmama the part she lived through that my grandmama didn't live through and my grandmama told my mama what they both lived through and my mama told me what they all lived through and we were suppose to pass it down like that from generation to generation so we'd never forget. Even though they'd burned everything to play like it didn't never happen." [p. 8]

In Ursa's great-grandmother's vision, one's children and one's children's children thus counter the fragmentation of time that is fostered by the white repudiation of the past.

In contrast to the destroyed written records, this oral account has an immediacy whose effect is to recreate the past as present reality, in which Ursa's mother *is* her own mother and grandmother, much as Okonkwo in *Things Fall Apart* mythically reincarnates Amalinze the Cat or Captain Blackman in Williams's novel becomes Crispus Attucks. History becomes myth as individual memory coalesces with the common experience of generations; as Ursa's mother recounts her grandmother's memories, she shifts to first person, making the account given seem not memory but immediate experience, herself at one with her own grandmother in a mythic recreation of time in which the past fuses with the present. Fathered by the slave owner for his own profit, the children of Corregidora celebrate their own birth and the birth of generations to come in order that he, and by implication all white people, may not burn the past. Birth, the outcome of rape and incest, is transmuted into cause for a celebration that redeems what was intended as a crucible of only shame and profit.

Corregidora includes another dimension of the ambiguities related to childbirth. Early in the novel, Ursa's husband pushes her down a flight of stairs, causing her to undergo a hysterectomy. Ursa's task is to reconcile a heritage that requires that she "make generations" with her own inability to do so. By the novel's end, Ursa has made multiple journeys through time. The first-person narrative moves forward through twenty-three years of Ursa's life, from 1947 to about 1970, and ranges backward as well to Ursa's own childhood, her mother's childhood and young womanhood, and to her grandmother's and great-grandmother's lives a century before. By the end of the novel, too, Ursa has also found in the songs she writes and sings an alternative means of ensuring the common fund of memory on which a continuity in time depends. When her mother accuses her of singing "devil" songs, asking her where she got them, Ursa replies that the songs come from the memories her mother has shared with her:

Yes, if you understood me, Mama, you'd see I was trying to explain it, in blues, without words, the explanation somewhere behind the words. To explain what will always be there. Soot crying out of my eyes; "O Mister who come to my house You do not come to visit You do not come to see me to visit You come to hear me sing with my thighs You come to see me open my door and sing with my thighs Perhaps you watch me when I am sleeping I don't know if you watch me when I am sleeping. Who are you? I am the daughter of the daughter of the daughter of Ursa of currents, steel wool and electric wire for hair. [pp. 74–75]

In *Corregidora*, as in works by DuBois, James Weldon Johnson, Attaway, Hurston, Ellison, and Baldwin, to name only a few, music embodies black heritage and the continuity of past with present. Ursa makes it clear that she does not sing primarily to support herself or to please men; rather, she sings for the same reason that her great-grandmother made sure that those who came after her would share her memories of the past. For Ursa, the blues become an act of rebellious celebration, equivalent to her great-grandmother's "making generations." For Gayl Jones, *Corregidora* offers an equivalent act of rebellious celebration, a novel that refuses to smooth over the ambiguities in recognizing that childbirth and motherhood figure as part of a heritage. Jones refuses to reduce Ursa Corregidora to a female type—a Woman—in order to achieve a resolution of the dualities implicit in the contingencies of black time.

In *Meridian* Alice Walker explores similar ambiguities of motherhood. As a young woman, the title character gives up her child after her husband has left her, in order to go to college and to continue an involvement in the civil-rights movement, then (1960) gaining momentum. Later she has an abortion, and is sterilized. Meridian twice refuses to be a Mother or a Woman, even though her refusal makes her regard herself "as belonging to an unworthy minority, for which there was no precedent and of which she was, as far as she knew, the only member" (p. 91). Much of the remaining narrative is devoted to correcting Meridian's perception that she is alone in a society that values children, as she learns of instance after instance of society's rejection and abuse of children.

Meridian's own mother would have preferred a childless life. "She could never forgive her community, her family, his family, the whole world, for not warning her against children. . . . She learned—much to her horror and amazement—that she was not even allowed to be resentful that she was 'caught' " (p. 50). Her metaphor for motherhood is being "buried alive, walled away from her own life, brick by brick" (p. 51). Yet she cannot conceive of not raising her children once she has them.

At college Meridian learns of Fast Mary, who "concealed her pregnancy and muffled her cries . . . as the child was being born," afterward chopping the newborn child "into bits" and trying to flush it down the toilet; but "the bits stuck and Fast Mary was caught," flogged, and locked in her room where, three months later, she hanged herself.

Meridian also comes to know Wild Child, a pregnant thirteen-year-old child of the streets whom no one claims and no one can catch. Meridian succeeds in bringing her to her room in the college honors house, only to be told that the child cannot stay in "a school for young ladies" (pp. 36–37). Wild Child escapes while Meridian is trying to find a school or home that will accept her: "Running heavily across a street, her stomach the largest part of her, she was hit by a speeder and killed" (p. 37).

Later, while registering people to vote in the South, she meets a dying woman who wants to be buried on Mother's Day and a young woman who has strangled her baby. During this time, too, six-year-old Camara, the daughter of her friends Lynne and Truman, is "attacked by a grown man" and dies. Still later, in a chapter entitled "Camara"—though the child herself is not mentioned—Meridian attends a church service. An aging, "red-eyed" man whose son had been killed some years before is brought forward and makes a three-word speech: "My son died" (p. 198). This incident follows another involving the death of a five-year-old boy drowned in a ditch neglected by city officials; before being "raked out with a grappling hook," the boy has been stuck in the sewer for two days.

In sum, Meridian discovers that she lives in a world where motherhood is linked with death, and the reader discovers the significance of the chapter title "Camara": in Meridian's growing vision, the death of the six-year-old Camara causes a "loss not unlike the loss of Martin Luther King or Malcolm X or George Jackson" (p. 174). The red-eyed man lost his son in the struggle for civil rights: but in a larger sense the deaths of all children signal martyrdom in a society "where children are not particularly valued" (p. 174). She comes to see the use of the vote as at least a small "resistance to the murder of [the] children" (p. 191). Later, she realizes that the red-eyed man's testimony has been a way for the community to "weave" the man's story into the songs and the sermons that sustain the church, which she defines as "the communal spirit, togetherness, righteous convergence" (p. 200). She comes to understand that "the respect she owed her life was to continue, against whatever obstacles, to live it, and not to give up any particle of it without a fight to the death, preferably *not* her own" (p. 200). Years before she had doubted her ability to kill "for the revolution" because she saw such killing as the abnegation of a cultural past, of "old black men in the South" and "young girls singing in a country choir . . . their voices the voices of angels" (p. 28). But following the red-eyed man's testimony, she vows that "yes indeed she *would* kill, before she allowed anyone to murder his son again" (p. 200).

Meridian's vision of motherhood becomes mythic, the death of one child a threat to all children, her vow to murder if necessary an affirmation of the value of children that defies the values of a world where children are most commonly victims. In Alice Walker's vision, this affirmation culminates a spiritual journey that began with Meridian's rejection of her own child. Unlike the novels by Baldwin, McKay, and Gaines, *Meridian* does not assume its central character's celebration of childbirth and motherhood; rather, the contingencies in the world faced by Tish, Bita Plant, and Jane Pittman are internal as well as external, not only a part of the world which Meridian inhabits but also a part of her own character. Moreover, Meridian does not resolve these contingencies by having a child or by taking care of someone else's child; she demonstrates a fierce commitment to remaking the world that fosters these contingencies into a place where children may thrive. Her ties are not with a man, a family, or even with a specific community; she sees her existence as inseparable from that of all black people, as extending "beyond herself to those around her because, in fact, the years in America had created them One Life" (p. 200). By the end of the

novel Meridian has attained a complexity that defies reduction
to a type, and shares with Ursa Corregidora a strength that differs from that of Baldwin's women, Bita Plant, and Miss
Pittman. The Woman and the Mother rebel against temporal
chaos by insisting on their archetypal identity as mythic cele-
brants, recognizing the contingencies of time that lie all about
them but refusing to embody what is extrinsic to the mythic
truth of a traditional past. By contrast, both Ursa Corregidora
and Meridian find the heritage that is the source of their common celebration large enough to accommodate the ambiguities
they carry within themselves. Their complexity reduces neither
their strength nor their capacity to celebrate that heritage.

A complexity similar to that of Ursa Corregidora and Meridian is suggested or achieved by a number of women characters in
black fiction who rebel against being Mules. But for the Mule
who rebels there is no guarantee of redemption. Margaret, in
Alice Walker's *The Third Life of Grange Copeland*, rebels: after
years of enduring the isolation, physical abuse, and infidelity
imposed on her by her husband—after years of being his
Mule—she takes a shotgun to him and extracts his promise to re-
form; and for a time he keeps his promise. Margaret's mother
rebels against being a Mule through infidelity with the white
Shipley; after her husband's subsequent desertion, she poisons
both herself and Shipley's sickly baby. Similarly, in *Blood on the
Forge*, Anna rebels against the poverty and downtrodden status
of being a poor farmer's wife, leaves, becomes a prostitute in the
nightmarish steel-mill town of the novel—and finds she has
only exchanged one burden for another. In *Native Son*, Bessie
rebels against Bigger only long enough to name him as her at-
tacker and Mary's murderer; then she dies.

In Gayl Jones's *Eva's Man*, Eva Medina's rebellion is recurrent—and unredemptive. She recounts her own story from a psy-
chiatric cell, where she has spent five years after poisoning her
lover, Davis, and biting off his penis. Davis had imprisoned
her in his room, and for Eva, murdering him is an act of rebellion against not only this imprisonment but all the various sexually oriented imprisonments that men have attempted to impose
on her. Beginning when her mother's lover attempted to force

her into sex, sexuality for Eva has meant entrapment, acquiescence to Mule status, and abnegation of self. A cousin also attempted to force her into sex, and the man she married was so jealous that he would not allow her to have a telephone. Eva has rebelled before, stabbing a man who tried to pay her for the sexual favors he expected—and as a result she was sent to prison. The cycle in which Eva is caught, of oppression and rebellion, of violence and imprisonment, mimes the familiar *ogbanje* cycle of destruction. It is Bigger's cycle in *Native Son* and Dinah's in *Children of Sisyphus*. At the novel's end, there is no indication that the cycle will be redeemed.

Janie Starks's rebellion in Hurston's *Their Eyes Were Watching God* is also recurrent, but redemptive. Janie twice rebels against being a Mule, only to find herself trapped in the very fate she had sought to elude, like Eva seemingly caught in a recurrent and destructive cycle. Ultimately, however, in the relationship Janie has with Tea Cake, the cycle is redeemed into the goodness of time. Her narrative begins when her grandmother informs her that the "nigger woman is de mule of de world" and is structured by her successive rebellions against such a fate—her marriage to Killicks, her elopement with Jody Starks, her relationship with Tea Cake. But it is also structured by a growth in Janie's vision, as she modifies her concept of what a Mule is, finally achieving an accuracy of vision at the point where she has, in the love she shares with Tea Cake, transcended her predicted fate.

Her first act of rebellion—her marriage to Killicks, a well-off farmer—has as its premise that the "burden" to be avoided is a material one of poverty and deprivation. She sees Killicks's farm as a kind of insurance and as a means to gain what her grandmother terms a "respectability" almost indistinguishable from that of the white "Mis' Washburn." Were Janie a Bita Plant, her story might well end at this point. But, unlike Bita, Janie is not a Woman; and without love and children, the Killickses' household is a divided one, the divisiveness of respectability equivalent to that of poverty. She finds that the "burden" of respectability, a value fostered by the white world, obviates any possibility of spiritual well-being. Estranged from Killicks, from love and any

sense of community, she has, like Ananse, gained an estrangement of spirit along with a full stomach. Though Killicks does
not physically mistreat her, he views her as a material possession
not unlike the mule with which he plows his fields; and their
marriage offers to Janie an imprisonment equivalent to Eva
Medina's.

In flight from a spiritually destructive respectability, Janie
runs off with Jody Starks. There seems a chance that respectability will be compatible with love as Starks becomes a store owner
and mayor in an all-black Florida town, a highly respected member of the community. The material deprivation that her grandmother warned against has apparently been eluded, and the
love that Starks and Janie initially share seems to negate the
spiritual estrangement of Janie's marriage to Killicks. Once
again, however, Janie finds that respectability and the material
well-being that it brings erode love, and that her relationship
with Starks has "left the bedroom and took to living in the
parlor." The estrangement between Janie and Starks is mirrored
in Janie's estrangement from the community. She lives in a
house with "two stories with porches, with bannisters and such
things. The rest of the town looked like servants quarters surrounding the 'big house.' " Instead of the redemptive union with
heritage and community experienced by Meridian and Ursa
Corregidora, Janie lives a life of isolation in the role of white
mistress of the "big house." The attempt to escape the past is re-
warded with its reenactment; and in Hurston's vision the twist is
that the assumption of a different role, one of power rather than
powerlessness, represents only a different manner of fragmentation of community and heritage. The Ananse-like collaboration with the white world suggested in her marriage to Killicks is,
in her status as Starks's wife, fulfilled.

Janie's discovery of this ironic recapitulation is implied some
time before Starks's death. In a comic chapter, the hangers-on at
Starks's store hold a mock funeral for a dead mule. Starks cannot understand their wasting time on such nonsense, and Janie
replies that some people enjoy having "fun." Symbolically the
burial is more than fun: Janie, like the real mule, has escaped be-

ing a Mule only through a kind of death. She has become estranged from her husband, from the community, from any redemptive sense of heritage. She has landed in No Man's Land for refusing to be a Mule.

At first, Tea Cake is important to Janie for what he is not—not interested in making money, not interested in respectability. The fun she has with him—fishing, playing checkers, going to a baseball game—is an antidote to death; and in the course of the narrative it becomes clear that Tea Cake's refusal of respectability is a part of his profound alliance with life. He and Janie become itinerant farm workers, and the sharing quality of their relationship becomes the focal point of a sense of community among the other workers. The former mayor's wife works in the fields alongside Tea Cake and the others, and late into the night they share food and festivities with the other workers. As the mayor's wife in the "big house," Janie was above the community; with Tea Cake she becomes a part of its strength and its celebration. Early in their relationship, Tea Cake has asked her if she means to "partake wid everything"; unlike Starks, he is more than willing to share his life. Tea Cake fosters Janie's redemption into time: mythically, in fostering her union with him and with the community, Tea Cake becomes a spiritual guide through whom Janie becomes a celebrant rather than a victim of time.

A flood sweeps through the community where Janie and Tea Cake are living. Though both escape, Tea Cake is bitten by a rabid dog. Later, insane with rabies, he attacks Janie; in order to save her own life, she kills him with a shotgun. Tea Cake literally dies in order that Janie may live; mythically, he becomes the sacrifice that ensures Janie's redemption into time. An observation made earlier in the novel becomes an appropriate epitaph: "Half gods are worshipped in wine and flowers. Real gods require blood" (p. 215).

The focus of Janie's story is marriage, but marriage becomes a vehicle of rebellion—first against being a Mule, then against being an inhabitant of No Man's Land. Mythically, it is a story of spiritual growth, of death, birth, and sacrifice. Ultimately, as the title implies, the focus of the novel's vision is a mythic god, a god whose strength can redeem the destructive cycle into the goodness of time.

Tea Cake may well be the first example in black fiction of what Toni Morrison terms the "free man"[22]—a man who refuses to find his redemption through a woman, who is complete in himself. The character whom Morrison cites from her own fiction is Ajax from *Sula*. The fatal attraction of such men may be that in not seeking to possess they do just that. Before meeting Ajax, Sula Peace is described as never sleeping with the same man twice, whatever plea he may make. Confronted with a man whose freedom equals her own, she falls victim to the need for possession that she has earlier scorned. Seeing this, Ajax leaves her. Tea Cake is equally free, different only because he finds a mode of love in which neither he nor Janie possesses the other, but in which both belong to a larger community and in their love celebrate this larger, essentially mythic union.

There are at least two important consequences to a black writer's creation of a woman character who exceeds a type. First, as she confronts the ambiguities within herself, she is by implication confronting not just the white world or the black world, but the contingencies that result from the opposition of the two. After her early childhood, Janie Starks is shown living in a world largely isolated from white people—Killicks's farm, the black Florida community, the community of itinerant farm laborers. But as Hurston is careful to demonstrate, spiritual contingencies are not resolved simply by isolation from an external reality, because that reality has come to dwell within: in achieving respectability, Janie fulfills the material values that, in Hurston's vision, belong to the white world. The past, which for Janie includes a childhood in which she did not at first recognize any difference between herself and the white children with whom she played, is not to be repudiated.

In a larger sense, the past includes not only the mythic unity of traditional Africa celebrated by the Woman and the Mother, but the contingencies of dispossession and temporal chaos.

22. Toni Morrison, "Intimate Things in Place," p. 174.

Though the Woman or the Mother may achieve a mythic strength of celebration, one that is not lightly to be dismissed, if her character does not embody the wholeness of her heritage—including the threat of dispossession and chaos—then in itself character implies a reduction of that heritage. Tish in *Beale Street*, for example, is reduced in a way that John Grimes in *Go Tell It on the Mountain* is not. John Grimes arrives at a wholeness of celebratory vision after working through the contingencies present in himself as well as in his world; Tish begins where John ends, and starts her first-person narrative with a certainty of her status as a Woman, as a mythic celebrant. The hazards that Tish recounts do not erode or bring into question this certainty.

Why did Baldwin not continue John Grimes's own story in *Beale Street*, since Tish embodies an extension of the vision he attains? Why does McKay not continue his practice of using men as central characters in *Banana Bottom*? And why is *The Autobiography of Miss Jane Pittman* centered on a woman, when Gaines earlier had emphasized men? At least in part, the answer is that all three writers found the strength implicit in the Woman or the Mother, in the female character type, useful for resolving the kinds of dualities raised but not entirely resolved in their earlier fiction. Rather than achieve this resolution by reducing a male character's ambiguities to the simplicity of the type, they have chosen to do so with women characters. In creating the Woman or the Mother, the novelist creates a Mule to resolve for him the contingencies of time.

A second consequence of the female character who transcends the type is a concomitant shift in the characterization of men. Male characters begin to emerge who do not need a Mule—unlike Egbo, or young Cholly Breedlove, or Bigger Thomas, or Fonny, or the Commandant of the *Reconnaissance*, or Jude Greene. In *Their Eyes Were Watching God* the result is Tea Cake, a man who has forged his own redemption and who is willing in turn to be Janie's guide to her redemption. In *Meridian* the result is Truman Held, a man who ultimately learns, with Meridian's help, that a woman is not a Mule and that the man who needs a Mule reduces not only the woman but himself. In

Corregidora the result is Mutt, a man who can wait a quarter of a century for Ursa Corregidora to work out her own relationship to time and then not ask her to work his out as well. In Toni Morrison's fiction, the results are multiple: Ajax in *Sula*, for example, and Milkman Dead and Guitar Bains in *Song of Solomon*. The result may not be pleasant: insofar as responsibility rests on their refusal either to possess or be possessed by a woman, both Ajax and Milkman are responsible for the deaths of the women who love them.

PART 3

FROM FRAGMENTATION TO REDEMPTION: SEVEN REPRESENTATIVE NOVELS

The seven novels discussed in Part 3 can be grouped as follows:

The Erosion of the Cycle: *Arrow of God; In the Castle of My Skin;* and *Cane*

No Man's Land: *Blood on the Forge* and *Why Are We So Blest?*

The Redemption of the Cycle: *Song of Solomon* and *Season of Anomy*

At the beginning of *Arrow of God*, the mythic cycle is intact, but predominantly, the novel chronicles its erosion, as do *In the Castle of My Skin* and *Cane*. In the world of *Blood on the Forge* and *Why Are We So Blest?* the mythic cycle belongs to the long-ago past, as the characters are confronted with the chaos of No Man's Land. In the final two novels, *Song of Solomon* and *Season of Anomy*, the attempt is to redeem time into its original cyclic integrity. Taken together, these seven novels offer an imaginative history of the black past and, perhaps, a mythic blueprint for the future.

Chinua Achebe, *Arrow of God*

In 1964, Nigeria had been independent from Britain for four years. The Biafran conflict had not yet begun. The Organization for African Unity had high hopes of effacing, at least in spirit, the artificial national boundaries drawn by the colonial powers of Europe some eighty years before at the Berlin Conference, where the "pie" of Africa had been divided. The year 1964 was the year when many newly independent African countries participated for the first time in the Olympic Games, held in Tokyo. The year before, W. E. B. DuBois had died in Ghana just at the moment when the Reverend Martin Luther King was leading the March on Washington that would culminate in his "I Have a Dream" speech. In many ways, it was a year of new beginnings in which the fulfillment of decades, even centuries, of hope seemed within reach at last.

It was during this year, when much of the world was looking forward to the future, that Achebe published *Arrow of God*, the second of two novels in which his avowed intent was to "repair the foundations of the past." The spirit of his concern was in part cautionary, a reminder that forces of history, the forces of progress, may also be the forces of disintegration, chaos, and dispossession. But *Arrow of God* is also a eulogy of sorts, in which Achebe charts the erosion of a traditionally conceived social order and mourns its passing. Ten years later—after the Biafran war, after coups and countercoups in Nigeria and elsewhere—he would admit that had he not written *Arrow of God* and *Things Fall Apart* when he did, they might never have been written. Their focus on the past separated them from the present reality, he remarked, from "the occult zone where the people dwell." If his assessment is true, then *Arrow of God* is doubly a product of the times: first, of the period when Ibo society underwent the radical changes that accompanied the intrusion of British colonialism and Christianity; and second, of the period—in retrospect, a brief moment of the early sixties—when the hope was extended that men of good will, having learned from the past, might restore a new sense of order and social unity. Perhaps now, more than fifteen years after *Arrow of God* was written, this restoration is once again in sight in Nigeria. But the price in human lives and social disruption has been high.

In *Arrow of God* Achebe begins by outlining for the reader how Umuaro was originally founded, making explicit as he does so the structure of traditional African society, in which spiritual and political concerns were unified rather than at odds, in which the unified community was the source of all strength, both spiritual and political. Threatened with destruction by a hostile community, six villages unite for the sake of their survival, the mode of their unification making it clear that effective warfare and spiritual unity are inseparable as they unite under the aegis of a single deity.

In the very distant past, when lizards were still few and far between, the six villages—Umuachala, Umunneora, Umuagu, Umuezeani, Umugwu-gwu and Umuisiuzo—lived as different people, and each worshipped its own deity. Then, the hired soldiers of Abam used to strike in the dead of night, set fire to houses and carry men, women and children into slavery. Things were so bad for the six villages that their leaders came together to save themselves. They hired a strong team of medicine-men to install a common deity for them. This deity which the fathers of the six villages made was called Ulu. Half of the medicine was buried at a place which became the Nkwo market and the other half thrown into the stream which became Mili Ulu. The six villages then took the name of Umuaro, and the priest of the Ulu became their Chief Priest. From that day they were never again beaten by an enemy. [p. 16]

Through their commission of the creation of Ulu, the people manifest the primacy of the human community in spiritual matters. The "medicine-men" become the mediators in this creation, but their power comes from the people. Similarly, once Ulu has been created, the priest of Ulu (Ezeulu) becomes the mediator between the people and their god. This reciprocal exchange is shown in figure 5. In this cyclic continuum of spiritual-political power, Ezeulu's power is not autonomous but resides in his relationship to his god and his people. As the priest of Ulu, he is the Keeper of Time in Umuaro, and on behalf of the people preserves the continuity of the cycle through a monthly ritual sacrifice, after each new moon roasting one of the thirteen ritual yams brought to him after the harvest and eating it on behalf of his god. When only one yam remains, he will call the harvest festival. Each month also, he makes a ritual announcement to the community that the new moon has arrived. He does not "own" time, he merely "keeps" it.

As the quoted passage indicates, the ritual obligations of the generations of priests of Ulu have borne political fruit: since the creation of Ulu and the installment of his priest, Umuaro has "never again been beaten by an enemy."

Ezeulu calls himself a "watchman" whose power is no greater than a child's "over a goat that was said to be his. As long as the

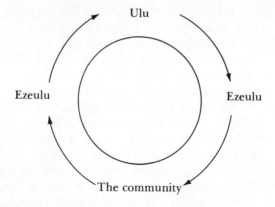

Figure 5

goat was alive it was his; he would find it food and take care of it. But the day it was slaughtered he would know who the real owner was" (p. 3). If the people should choose to destroy Ulu, as they have created him, Ezeulu would find himself powerless.

The central duality in the novel, however, is that Ezeulu's vision is at odds with the role he has been given. Knowing that the origin of his power, like that of his god's, lies with the people, he is nevertheless galled when he ponders this and in his thoughts rebels against the notion that his power is "no more than the power in the anus of the proud dog who tried to put out a furnace with his puny fart" (p. 4).

> No! the Chief Priest was more than that, must be more than that. If he should refuse to name the day there would be no more festival—no planting and no reaping. But could he refuse? No Chief Priest had ever refused. So it could not be done. He would not dare.
>
> Ezeulu was stung to anger by this as though his enemy had spoken it.
>
> "Take away that word *dare*," he replied to this enemy, "Yes I say take it away. No man in all Umuaro can stand up and say that I dare not. The woman that will bear the son who will say it has not yet been born" (p. 3).

The remainder of the novel is taken up with moving the contradiction between his role and his vision from the realm of the hypothetical to the real, to a battle in which Ezeulu's antagonists —and thus duality in the novel—increase to include the community of Umuaro itself, the British colonial government, the Christian missionaries, his own son Oduche, Ezedimili (the priest of the sacred python), and his own god. For reasons that the intervening narrative make clear, he announces that the harvest will not take place until two additional months have passed, though he and everybody else recognize that this will mean famine. He has decided to fit his role to the demands of his vision, and symbolically he attempts to stop time, to imprison it in his own vision of what it should be. The implication of his decision is the disruption of cyclic time, and disaster.

Three episodes in the narrative foreshadow Ezeulu's final decision to pit his own vision against the power and welfare of the community: a land dispute with the neighboring community of

Okperi; Oduche's imprisonment of the sacred python; and his own imprisonment by the colonial government.

The land dispute has begun some five years before the novel opens. Ezeulu infuriates Umuaro by siding with Okperi, apparently in the sincere belief that they have right on their side. Umuaro overrides Ezeulu's objections, sending emissaries to Okperi to discuss the issue further. Akukalia, an impotent man who gives his wives to other men in order to get children, becomes infuriated when an Okperi man calls him a "castrated bull" (p. 20) and retaliates by destroying the man's ancestral shrine—making the man a "corpse" in spiritual terms, cut off from the regenerative spiritual cycle much as Akukalia himself is. Okperi avenges this desecration by killing Akukalia, and the land dispute flares into a war between the two communities that continues until Captain Winterbottom brings soldiers to end it and, by seizing the guns in the two villages, to prevent its recurrence. Later, colonial officials sit in judgment on the land dispute and award the land to Okperi.

In this episode, Ezeulu has asserted his vision against the opinion of Umuaro. Humiliated when his advice is defied, he is as galled at the insult to his power as Akukalia is by the denigration of his manhood. Yet in the outcome there is a tentative vindication of Ezeulu's vision: the acquisitiveness of Umuaro has resulted in loss of life, the desecration of a shrine that embodies cyclic continuity, and the intervention of Winterbottom. Ezeulu's vision, seemingly at odds with the material welfare of the village, has proven pragmatically right.

Three years after this incident, Ezeulu sends his son Oduche to be his "ears" at the Christian mission, saying, "If there is nothing in it, you will come back. But if there is something there you will bring home my share. The world is like a Mask dancing. If you want to see it well you do not stand in one place" (p. 51). Oduche's mother is unhappy that her son has been chosen as a "sacrifice" to the white man, but Oduche goes and by the time the novel opens has become not a spy but a convert. One of the missionaries urges him to test his new faith: "You address the python as Father. It is nothing but a snake, the snake that deceived our first mother, Eve. If you are afraid to kill it, do not count yourself a Christian" (p. 52). A few days later, as Oduche prepares to smash the python's head, he hears someone coming and locks the python in a wooden box. "He felt a great relief within. The python would die for lack of air, and he would be responsible for its death without being guilty of killing it" (p. 56). The python's struggles draw the attention of the other members of the family, however, and when Ezeulu breaks open the box and discovers the sacrilege his son has committed he swears he will kill Oduche "with his own hands" (p. 60).

Oduche's conversion, like the Umuaroan defiance in the land dispute, is a betrayal of Ezeulu's vision, with similar effect. The British invade Umuaro with their God this time rather than their soldiers—Ezeulu's "share" of Christianity is a desecration of the sacred cycle equivalent to Akukalia's desecration of the shrine. The priest of the sacred python blames Ezeulu for abomination to his god, and the village mocks him for what his contact with Christianity has brought.

Midway in the narrative Ezeulu, summoned to Winterbottom's colonial headquarters in Okperi, refuses the summons, saying that the white man knows where to find him. For this impertinence and, later, for his refusal of the warrant chieftainship which Winterbottom offers him, Ezeulu is imprisoned. There is a two-month-long hiatus in his sacrificial offerings to Ulu before he is finally released. Ezeulu refuses to call the harvest when the yams are ripe in the field, and explains to the elders of Umuaro: "You all know what our custom is. I only call a new festival when there is only one yam. Today I have three yams and so I know that the time has not come" (p. 236). Until the sacrificial cycle interrupted by his imprisonment has been completed, there will be no harvest. Ezeulu's motivations for this refusal, however, are more complex than he lets on.

In part, his motivation springs from impotence. Overridden by Umuaro in the land dispute with Okperi, made a fool by his son's imprisonment of the python, and held by the British for several weeks, he is enraged at this seemingly multiple conspiracy to deprive him of his authority as priest. Like the impotent Akukalia, he strikes back at those who have insulted him, and the effect of his decision would be to turn all of Umuaro into corpses—literally, since the yams will rot in the fields as the people starve.

But his motivation is also a test of his faith and of his vision. Ezeulu's decision is not finally made until after he has a vision in which Ulu tells him that the refusal is necessary because it will put his rival deity, Idemili, in his place. The god says, "Beware you do not come between me and my victim or you may receive blows not meant for you. . . . Leave me to settle my quarrel with Idemili, who wants to destroy me so that his python may come to power. . . . As for me and Idemili, we shall fight to the finish" (p. 219). Following this vision, Ezeulu sees himself as "no more than an arrow in the bow of his god." Like his son's imprisonment of the python, Ezeulu's symbolic acquiescence to the imprisonment of time is a testimony to the power of his god.

Following this vision, too, Ezeulu reassesses Oduche's sacrilege and the white man's imprisonment of himself. Perhaps Oduche's imprisonment of the python came as part of Ulu's struggle against Idemili; perhaps Oduche is also "an arrow in the hand of Ulu" (p. 219). Perhaps the white man is as well, since by exiling Ezeulu he has given him "a weapon with which to fight his enemies" (p. 222). In this reassessment, Ezeulu has found a way to accommodate his role and his vision with no contradiction. He does this by defining both in terms of his god rather than in terms of the people. He has reversed the terms of his initial musing that the people own the god, like a goat, and that he is only a watchman of the god for the people—instead he asserts the god's predominance.

The implications of Ezeulu's reassessment are both material and spiritual, and both turn upon the damage that has been done to the cyclic ideal. Ezeulu has a certain awareness of the material consequences: "What troubled him most—and he alone seemed to be aware of it at present—was that the punishment [of Ulu] was not for now alone but for all time. It would afflict Umuaro like an *ogulu-aro disease* which counts a year and returns to its victims" (p. 250). His imprisonment of time is not a discrete act of present time, but for all time. For Umuaro, much as for the *ogbanje* child, cyclic recurrence will embody a recurrent fatality rather than renewal. This fatality implies, too, that the cycle itself has been broken. No longer will time run according to the seasons but according to the demands of a willful god: it becomes the property of the spiritual world. Implicit in this is that the god himself becomes absolute, no longer to be created or destroyed by the people for their benefit—the god will be impervious to human need except as this need accords with his own divine pattern. Sacrifice will no longer proceed from the human community as a part of their manipulation of the spiritual world. It will be an imperative imposed from above—the sacrifice in this instance of the entire yam crop. Of Abraham, God demanded only Isaac. From Ezeulu he seems to demand an entire community.

Ezeulu has placed his god at the top of a hierarchical linear relationship, as shown in figure 6. The structure of power becomes linear, without the reciprocity implicit in the cycle of the ideal. The cycle destroyed, political and spiritual disaster soon follow, manifested in an event that occurs shortly after Ezeulu's announcement.

Ezeulu's eldest son, Obika, rises from his sickbed to participate in a funeral ritual, circling around the villages of Umuaro in an apparent ritual mime of the passage of the dead man's soul to the world of spirits. As he completes his cyclic journey, Obika falls dead at his original starting point. In symbolic terms, his

Figure 6

death is the death of the cycle itself—as Ezeulu puts it, the "ruin of all things":

Why, he asked himself again and again, why had Ulu chosen to deal thus with him, to strike him down and cover him with mud? What was his offence? Had he not divined god's will and obeyed it? When was it ever heard that a child was scalded by the piece of yam its own mother put in its palm? What man would send his son with a potsherd to bring fire from a neighbor's hut and then unleash rain on him? Who ever sent his son up the palm to gather nuts and then took an axe and felled the tree? But today such a thing had happened before the eyes of all. What could it point to but the collapse and ruin of all things? [p. 206]

Though Ezeulu perhaps has realized that his vision implied an arbitrary god—a god who could remake time—he did not realize that this arbitrariness could be visited upon himself. The people of Umuaro see in Obika's death their own vindication: "Their god had taken sides with them against his headstrong and ambitious priest and thus upheld the wisdom of their ancestors—that no man however great was greater than his people; that no man ever won judgment against his clan" (p. 261). This is only part of the truth. The reader realizes, too, what Ezeulu only partly recognizes: that no priest however great is greater than an absolute god. Ezeulu's tragedy is that, in remaking the reciprocity of the cycle into a linear absolute, he has unwittingly collaborated in his own destruction.

Though many critics have taken sides with Umuaro, viewing the book as a vindication of the wisdom of the people, the concluding passage of the novel confirms that this is only a partial truth. For if it is true, as Umuaro sees it, that Ulu has taken sides with them against Ezeulu, then:

Ulu had chosen a dangerous time to uphold this wisdom. In destroying his priest he had also brought disaster on himself. . . . For a deity who chose a time such as this to destroy his priest or abandon him to his enemies was inciting people to take liberties; and Umuaro was just ripe to do so. The Christian harvest which took place a few days after Obika's death saw more people than even Goodcountry [one of the missionaries] could have dreamed. In his extremity many an Umuaro man had sent his son with a yam or two to offer the new religion and to bring back the promised immunity [from the possible wrath of Ulu]. Thereafter any yam that was harvested in the man's field was harvested in the name of the son. [pp. 261–62]

Though the people have supposedly seen Obika's death as a sign that Ezeulu was wrong in delaying the harvest, their actions here grant the possibility that Ezeulu's decision had Ulu's sanction. Given that possibility, they abandon Ulu for the protection of the Christian church. As in their creation of Ulu, the people of Umuaro adopt a new god because of an urgent circumstantial need.

This new covenant with Christianity, however, is a mockery of the original covenant between Umuaro and Ulu. Fragmentation rather than unity becomes the means to material survival. The new religion is accepted by individuals acting in their individual interests. No community meeting is held, no unified community blessing of the sacrificial yams is given. The presentation of these yams, instead of the proud thing it had been, becomes a half-shameful act, eschewed by the elders, who send their children. The meaning of sacrifice is reduced to something like an individual business transaction, a "payment" for survival, and Christianity is thus portrayed as a "social organization . . . demanding payment for the symbols of membership."[1] Symbolically, cyclic time and the cyclic power structure that it implies have become the sacrificial victims in the establishment of the new covenant; the spiritual is sacrificed for the sake of the material. The missionaries have confiscated the yams much as the soldiers in the land dispute took away the guns; and the war within Umuaro among gods, priests, and the people has again been resolved through the intervention of Western imperatives. The yam fields now belong to the Son.

Acting from a sense of impotence, Ezeulu looks to his god for the power that his people have partially denied him. He becomes the sacrificial victim of his own god, but ironically, he has also become an "arrow" of Christ, insofar as he has become the symbolic murderer of Ulu—"responsible for [his] death, without being guilty of killing [him]." Nevertheless, implicit in the con-

---

1. J. B. Schuyler, SJ, "Conceptions of Christianity in the Context of Tropical Africa," p. 220.

clusion is an ambiguous vindication of Ezeulu's vision. Ezeulu has demonstrated willingness to defend a traditional god even, if necessary, to the death. He is wrong not in this demand, but in his implicit severance of the spiritual world from the world of natural process. In the numerous "imprisonments" of the novel, the power of Winterbottom and of British influence becomes generally clear. Directly or indirectly, the British have "imprisoned" the guns of Umuaro, the sacred python, the keeper of cyclic time, and the yams that symbolize both the political power of the people and their spiritual well-being. In sum, the British have imprisoned cyclic time, with the collaboration of Umuaro itself. Nothing less than Ezeulu's absolute affirmation of a traditional god could suffice to restore what has been violated. Before Ezeulu makes his demand, however—given the belief system, perhaps before he *can* make his demand—the fragmentation of cyclic structure has already begun, and in this context his vision becomes the vehicle of its own destruction.

Arrow of God provides the symbolic framework for understanding much of black fiction: the good life exists within a unified community, in which material blessing and spiritual sanctions are also unified. At the center of these values is a concept of time that implies both perpetual renewal and perpetual responsibility. In *Arrow of God*, as the leader becomes divorced from the community, human responsibility fails and the cycle is broken. The ideal presented in *Arrow of God* at the beginning of the novel is the ideal toward which black writers look: some of them imaginatively reconstruct it, while others chronicle the fragmentation and chaos of No Man's Land, the result of the erosion of the cycle.

George Lamming,
In the Castle of My Skin

George Lamming's first novel, *In the Castle of My Skin*, is a novel of both nostalgia and disillusionment. Set in the Barbados of the nineteen-thirties and forties, it charts a young boy's growth to manhood, but it charts as well the disintegration of a society in which at the beginning of the novel there are still glimpses of the African ideal of the continuum of time. In other novels as diverse as *Great Expectations* and *Manchild in the Promised Land*, the society within which the young person moves remains fixed, the search for identity occurring within a static world. In Lamming's novel the world itself is in a state of flux, and the young boy's growth from the stability of childhood to the uncertainties of being a man coincides with a chaotic movement in the world he inhabits. This duality of self and world coincides with a duality of time that mimes the historic antagonism between myth and history. By the conclusion of the novel, the boy has grown to maturity and myth has given place to dispossession.

The duality of time in the boy's world is embodied in the characters of Pa and Mr. Slime. Pa functions in the novel as the Keeper of Time, his mythic vision uniting Africa with the islands of the Caribbean as he recalls when life proceeded in concord with the cycle of the seasons: "Time was when I see by the sun how the season sail and the moon make warning what crops to expect. Leaf fall or blood stain by the edge of the sea was a way of leaving one thing for another" (p. 232). In memory and in dream, he re-creates a heritage and the subjugation of that heritage by European slave ships when "the silver of exchange cross the sea and my people scatter like clouds in the sky" and silver comes to mean more than "what pass from hand to hand. 'Tis also a way of what you call gettin' on" (p. 233). He sees, too, that present problems recapitulate that slave ship intrusion: "if the islands be sick, 'tis for no other reason than the ancient silver" (p. 233). The silver of the slave master has become, in the present, the silver that Slime is acquiring through embezzlement of the people's Penny Bank, using the money to buy their land from under them and ultimately evicting them. Pa sees that the spiritual unity of a world in which "star speak nothing but a world outside our world and the two was one" (p. 232) has been murdered by the corrupt politics of Slime. At the end, Pa is sent to the almshouse, he and his vision dispossessed from the land and from time.

The boy's own narrative counterpoints the interplay between Pa's vision and Slime's politics. Each is given his own narrative voice, narrative fragmentation miming that of society and time. Narrative structure also creates an ironic discrepancy between the boy's growth in vision and the changed world on which that vision must focus. The novel falls clearly into three parts: the boy's childhood, his early adolescence, and his young maturity. Each part begins with the boy's narration from a first-person point of view for a chapter or two; then point of view shifts to a third-person alternation between Slime and Pa. Focus on Pa is intensified as the narrative progresses, paralleling the boy's deepening intimacy with Pa. Simultaneously, as the boy comes closer to the unified vision that Pa affirms, that vision is disintegrating, though neither of them is aware of it. Just as the boy becomes fully aware of Pa's vision, Slime's corruption is made manifest to the entire village as the eviction notices arrive. As the boy grows toward a vision of the continuity of time, it is in the process of disintegration; his achieved vision coincides with the actuality of dispossession. A closer look at the three stages of the boy's life shows also three stages in his vision of time.

In the opening passage, the boy describes the moment between daylight and darkness when his mother lights the kerosene lamp:

> She lit the big brass lamp that hung from a beam riding the slopes of the ceiling. The space of the ceiling directly over the lamp wore a surface of soot. The lamp swayed in its cradle of wire, a bowl of polished brass, as the flames sputtered along the blue burnt edge of the wick. Standing beneath the flowered brass bowl that contained the fuel, my mother regulated the pitch of the blaze. The smoke circled the flames within the chimney and later settled on the wet ceiling. The light pushed its way about the corners of the house and the partitions in their dying response looked a dismal wreck in reflection. It was the uncertain light one feels on the passage from sleep to conscious waking. The clock shelved in one corner kept up its ticking. My mother retreated to another part of the house where the silk and taffeta designs of her needling were being revised and reversed. I soon followed like a lean trail of smoke tracing a radius round its red origin. [p. 4]

It is this smoky ambience of vision that defines the first two chapters of the book. The vision here is one of isolated moments—his mother lights the lamp, a pet pigeon dies, he is bathed by his mother, a friend receives a beating. Only toward the end of the second chapter does he attempt to connect these isolated moments to the world that exists outside his mother's house, and here too there is a disconnection among details: the overseer's house high on the hill, an old woman urinating by a tree, a naked couple making love in the public bathhouse. For the boy, the world is caught in the murky light that accompanies the flood at the beginning of the novel; and, though in this ambience of the moment halfway between "sleep and consciousness" he has a perception of isolated images, isolated moments, they are beads on an invisible string, their continuity lost in images of smoke and dusk and fog.

Between this portion of the boy's narrative and the next there is a lengthy hiatus (three chapters, some one hundred pages) in which point of view becomes omniscient and the focus alternates between Slime (chapters 4 and 6) and Pa (chapter 5). Five years pass, during which the boy has disappeared both as character and narrator, as though his life, like the moments of his perception, embodies an inherent disjuncture void of continuity. But at midpoint in the novel he reappears and we see him engaged in boyish adventures with his friends Trumper, Boy Blue, and Bob. The center of his world—"its red origin"—is no longer his mother but his friends. Their adventures take them into the larger world of the village bound on one side by the landlord's hilltop house and on the other by the sea. Chapter 6 recounts the boys' day together at the beach and includes two near drownings, an encounter with a heroic fisherman, and numerous stories and anecdotes exchanged among the boys. Chapter 7 centers on the boys' nighttime clandestine and forbidden excursion to the landlord's house where from the bushes they spy on the party taking place within. The episode is framed by their involvement with a religious gathering at the outskirts of the village. They deride the gathering, but upon their return it provides refuge from the irate landlord's servants. Metaphorically, the boys' two excursions—one by day, the other by night—are an exploration of the boundaries of their world.

Here, too, the narrator captures the essence of an isolated moment, most vividly perhaps in those scenes which describe a certain cast of light reflected on the sea.

A wave shot forward right up to the line of our footprints in the sand. When the water slid back the sand sloped sharply to the sea, and the foam of the wave making brief bubbles over the sand shaped itself between the spaces of our toes. It formed a pattern that looked like a honeycomb after the bees had deserted the hive. The space between the bubbles was clear and distinct like a hole. We kept our toes still and watched the bubbles burn crystal in the sun till the wind blew them into the sand that slid back into the sea. The foam was very pretty, and quite different from the foam one saw floating over the surface of molasses. The bright brittle look of the sea-foam was soothing with the wind settled in the trees and then steadying itself to a tide that rippled along the level of the water. Silence was there again, hanging over the trees and the sea and falling through and over the flow of the wind. [p. 135]

The focus has shifted from the shadows to the sunshine, from domestic life to the expanse of the sea, but the boy's fourteen-year-old vision seems to embody very much the same quality as it did when he was nine. A closer look, however, shows some differences.

In both of these chapters, the boy's first-person-participant narration shifts to a sense of first-person observer; though it is clear the boy is involved in the action he describes, the focus is often entirely on Trumper, Blue Boy, and Bob. There is another shift, from first-person singular to plural, from "I" to "we." These shifts embody the boy's groping attempt to define his relation to the world and other people. He moves from an intimate but isolated perception of the sea—"I looked around me, and sniffing the salt air from my nostrils, ran to meet the tumble of the sea along the shore" (p. 119)—to an identification of his own perception and action with that of the other boys, implied in the passage above and more explicit elsewhere: "We looked at the sand and the sea and it seemed we could see the gradations of light. . . . We watched [a fisherman]. . . . We were silent" (p. 128). Moreover, interspersed in chapter 6 is a lengthy section in which the boy becomes a spectator, a listener, as Trumper relates a long anecdote of a villager caught in having promised to marry two girls at the same time on the same day. The shifts from "I" to "we" to the sense of his being an observer embody a recognition of his own identity as existing in a state of flux that mimes the chaos of the world around him. He is both apart from and part of the larger group, and he gropes to delineate the shifting boundaries between self and society.

Moreover, the boys' discussion signifies a view of time that diverges from that of chapters 1 and 2. Trumper remarks,

'Tis always like this. . . . I mean the way we is here. . . . 'Tis always like this at home the way we is here. My mother over yonder in that corner, an' my father down there in that corner, an' me somewhere else. An' you get the feelin', you know, that everything's all right. 'Cause of the way everybody sittin', just sittin' there, an' for the moment you feel nothin' ever change. Everything's all right, 'tis the same yesterday an' today an' tomorrow an' forever as they says in the Bible. [pp. 128–29]

At such a moment, as Boy Blue puts it, it is "as if time like the clock itself stop" (p. 130).

The boyish adventures in chapters 6 and 7 are islands of time amid the surrounding flux, attempts to fix and thereby define time. As Trumper and Boy Blue, and the narrator with them, perceive, the individual moment and the individual perception

have become stays against the chaos of the change that they inhabit. Earlier, when the boy described his mother lighting the
lamp, "the clock ticked on"; here, it stops. Earlier, he saw the
moment not as a moment; but as time itself. His vision of time
did not, could not, go beyond the isolated moment. Here, at
midpoint in the book, the narrator has grown in his awareness of
the societal chaos set in motion by Slime; the boy's yearning to
stay time, to halt the rush toward fragmentation, is at the thematic center of the novel. Faced with flux, the boys become conscious of stasis; faced with death (societal as well as individual),
they discover the concept of immortality. That their yearning is
futile, their discovery to no avail, is the burden of the third and
final portion of the novel.

The third portion of the boy's narration, which begins in
Chapter 11, opens with a vision of the lack of connection between isolated moments, a vision of pure flux. Another three
years have passed and the boy, now seventeen, is on the verge of
departure for Trinidad, where he will take up a teaching position. He discovers that a pebble he had hidden near the beach
the preceding day has disappeared, and his meditation on this
disappearance comprises a meditation on time gone mad in its
fragmentation.

The surface of the sand seemed much the same the day before, even,
sloping and undisturbed. I watched it as though there was an image of
the other day which I carried to check the details of this. But only that
day had passed and the pebble had gone. . . . I placed the pebble under
the grape leaf, left it to wait my return the next morning. . . . I knew it,
shape, size, and texture. I had held it long and seen it closely before
putting it away. And on the spot where I had placed it I had seen it
more accurately against the bed of sand. For a moment I wondered
whether the waves had washed up overnight, but I couldn't see why that
should have happened. The spot which I had chosen was far up the
shore. The sea was still the morning I hid the pebble and it was as still
this morning. Moreover, the sea on this side never ran so far up the
shore. I had no overwhelming sense of the supernatural, but I was
getting a strange feeling that something had interfered. I didn't know
how to relate the situation because I didn't know how I should describe
this sense of the other's interference. And in any case no one might
have cared to understand why I should have hidden the pebble at all. It

seemed rather silly when I thought of telling somebody, and since it was incommunicable to another I got the feeling more acutely of the other's interference. Either the pebble had taken itself away or something had lifted it from beneath the leaves. It was clear that the sea had played no part. There was nothing I could do but carry the feeling of the other's interference and resign myself to the loss. . . . I told myself that it was useless to search. The day before I had seen the pebble for the last time. [pp. 235–37]

The placement of the pebble and the attempt to find it the following day are a test of time, an effort to determine its continuity. It is as though the past moments of the boy's life have disappeared, as faces vanish when one views them from a speeding train. The individual moment as a stay against time becomes a childish illusion. The continuity of time is destroyed in the linear flux. It is in this episode that he grows aware of his own estrangement from time, time as "the other," the ultimate antagonist. Unlike the man in *The Beautyful Ones*, he finds the sea symbolic of chaos rather than of continuity.

In the following chapter, also narrated by the boy, Pa reiterates his belief that, despite the "sickness" of time, "there be things which remain

what they be, an' there ain't no changin' them. Do what you like, 'tis got to be what it is. Come rain come sun the day goes on. . . . Whatever Mr. Slime might do . . . there be nothing he can do to make the landlord other than what he is. . . . An' Mr. Slime will go on doin' what he doin', and we all livin' as we livin'." [p. 257]

The old man asserts the existence of a small-core continuity within the flux, a continuity that would counter the boy's sense of fragmentation. But at this point Slime has not yet dispossessed the villagers from the land—that is the subject of the following chapter. And when we encounter Pa for the last time, in the scene that concludes the book, his vision has finally been destroyed. The narrator and Pa meet each other late at night in the middle of the village; each is taking a last look around before his departure, the narrator to Trinidad and a teaching position, the old man to the almshouse. Pa summarizes the catastrophes: " 'The flood wus the beginnin' o' so much in this place. 'Twus strike an' then 'twus riot an' what with one rumour an' a next, now 'tis the land. We see Penny Bank and Society an' now 'tis the end' " (p. 34). The significance of all this is that when asked by the narrator what he thinks about Slime, Pa replies, " 'I don't know. . . . A man make a promise an' a man change, an' the man who make a promise ain't the same said man as the man who change, an' I don't know, I don't know who got the right to judge why he change or whether he should have change at all. I don't know' " (p. 341). Fragmentation has replaced Pa's vision of continuity. With the villagers' dispossession and the narrator's departure, the public and the personal threads of Lamming's narrative merge and embody a final estrangement from the land and the cyclic ideal that in Pa's vision the land represents. The vision itself is bankrupt and will be sent to the almshouse. The Keeper of Time is as good as dead, murdered by those who claim ownership by virtue of their silver.

Jean Toomer, *Cane*

Because most novels tell a story, they manifest a linear sequence. The sequence may be disrupted, turn back on itself or leap forward, but all these metaphors imply that a novel is something like a road, with detours, switchbacks, and shortcuts.

Jean Toomer's *Cane* is one of the exceptions. And in being an exception, in exempting itself from the constraints of linear structure, it is peculiarly appropriate to Toomer's intention in writing it:

> There was a valley, the valley of "Cane," with smoke-wreaths during the day and mist at night. A family of back-country Negroes had only recently moved into a shack not too far away. They sang. And this was the first time I'd ever heard the folk-songs and spirituals. They were very rich and sad and joyous and beautiful. But I learned that the Negroes of the town objected to them. They called them "shouting." They had victrolas and player-pianos. So, I realized with deep regret, that the spirituals, meeting ridicule, would be certain to die out. With Negroes also the trend was towards the small town and then towards the city—and industry and commerce and machines. The folk-spirit was walking in to die on the modern desert. That spirit was so beautiful. Its death was so tragic. Just this seemed to sum life up for me. And this was the feeling I put into "Cane." "Cane" was a swansong. It was a song of an end.[2]

Cane is the record of a dying, a record of the process rather than the end result. It has no climax at which one can say, "At last, the finality of death." It

2. Darwin T. Turner, Introduction to *Cane*, p. xxii.

is a novel built on the tension between the "folk-spirit" and "the machine." Death must come. The ultimate victory of the machine is inevitable, but this victory lies beyond the scope of the work itself. The tension is presented whole in the first vignette, "Karintha," the final drama, "Kabnis," and in each of the poems and stories between. It is a novel without resolution, with tension suspended throughout in a sustained scream. Its virtue lies in its refusal to release the tension.

Structurally, *Cane*'s parts represent not linear development but mythic recurrence. Each story, each poem, is simultaneously at its symbolic center. To give preeminence to any specific story or poem is to distort the achievement of *Cane*—the mythic portrayal of a mythic truth on the verge of destruction. Symbolically, it is the reiterated portrayal of the moment that flickers between one's certainty of doom and doom itself, or in the traditional West African concept of death, the time between the body's death and the spirit's return to the world of the ancestors—a moment of twilight suspension, in which death is implicit but not yet complete. In Toomer's metaphor it is the moment of the cane field, where "time and space have no meaning. . . . No more than the interminable stalks" (p. 11). The achievement of *Cane* is that it stays time, suspending total dispossession, at the moment in which the resolution into doom is most imminent. It is a nexus of time in which one misstep will set the linear clock ticking; Lamming's pebble will disappear, Okonkwo will behead the messenger, Bigger will kill the rat, the rabid dog will bite Tea Cake, the *Reconnaissance* will embark for San Cristobal.

The suspension of time is achieved and conveyed in part through the pervasiveness of a symbolic half-light—half-tones of mist, fog, firelight, dusk, smoke, candlelight, moonlight, and sunset that now flare briefly, now settle into darkness. Whether it is the countryside of Georgia or the asphalt streets of Chicago or Washington, D.C., it is this diffused light that dominates and thereby unifies the diversity of stories, vignettes, sketches, prose poems, poetry, and drama that comprise *Cane*.

Karintha "carries beauty like dusk on the eastern horizon," and the smoke that curls up from the smouldering "pyramidal sawdust pile" where she has buried her dead baby "spreads itself out over the valley, . . . so heavy you tasted it in water" (p. 2). For years, the only evidence of Becky's presence is the "thin wraith of smoke" that "curls up from the leaning chimney" (p. 6). When the chimney caves in, the smoke is only replaced by dust. In "Carma," a long parenthetical description is given over to the passage between sunset and moonlight:

The sun is hammered to a band of gold. Pine-needles, like mazda, are brilliantly aglow. . . . Smoke curls up, marvelous web spun by the spider sawdust pile. Curls up and spreads itself pine-high above the branch, a single silver band along the eastern valley. . . . Dusk takes the polish from the rails. Lights twinkle. . . . Torches flare. . . . Foxie, the bitch, slicks back her ears and barks at the rising moon. [p. 11]

Fern is wooed by the narrator of her story as "dusk . . . settled with a purple haze about the cane." The narrator goes on: "I felt strange, as I always do in Georgia, particularly at dusk. I felt that things unseen to men were tangibly immediate. It would not have surprised me had I had a vision" (p. 17). A vision does come to King Barlo (in "Esther") as "the town bell strikes six. The sun slips in behind a heavy mass of horizon cloud" (p. 20). As he labors in his vision, "dusk is falling rapidly, and the customary store lights fail to throw their feeble glow across the gray dust and flagging of the Georgia town" (p. 21). The fantasy that Esther weaves around King Barlo for the next sixteen years is set always at that moment when "the low evening sun sets the windows of McGregor's notion shop aflame" (p. 22), and when she finally confronts Barlo it is midnight but "she thinks that the windows are a dull flame" (p. 24). And it is under the "omen," the "spell" of a "blood-burning" moon that Tom Burwell is burned: "Torches were flung into the pile. A great flare muffled in black smoke shot upward" (p. 35).

In this shadowed haze of wraiths of smoke men and women aspire to realize their desires, their disillusionment or destruction veiled and softened by the haze. Though these half-tones flicker on a moment of almost incessant activity, often apocalyptic in nature, their effect is to weave human mutability into a larger cycle of mythic recurrence. There is an even more primary tension in *Cane*, one that subsumes the tension between the "folk-spirit" and the "machine"—the tension between myth and the timelessness of dispossession. Dispossession coexists with the mythic cycle. In these six stories, which comprise the first section of *Cane*, this half-light of dusk and moonlight has the consistent force of enchantment, of a time of visions, juju men, witch-doctors, dreams, and violence. For a flickering instant, the Dixie Pike becomes "a goat path in Africa," Karintha the reincarnation of Mammy-Wattah, and King Barlo the African slave of his visions. At this instant, the unity of human affairs with the mythic cycle is not illusory: but it is almost immediately shattered, and the pathos of many of these men and women is that they attempt to prolong the moment beyond its flickering span. It is the prolonging of the moment, not its flickering actuality, that constitutes illusion. Men would wish Karintha eternally innocent. Esther sees King Barlo as forever possessed by the sacred vision that he lost almost as soon as he gained it. Louisa believes Tom Burwell will come to see her as he always has, refusing to hear his final death-cry. In each of these stories Toomer presents a moment that, though it can be seized, cannot be held.

The second section of *Cane* begins with "Seventh Street," a prose poem in which images of blood and smoke are fused: "black reddish blood . . . swirling like a blood-red smoke up where the buzzards fly in heaven" (p. 39). In this section, set in the city, half-tones of moonlight and sunset are intermingled with the garish glow and shadows of neon, streetlights, and footlights. Here, too, the light is symbolically partial in focus: faces and heads leap out from shadowed landscapes and bodies that remain in darkness. Rhobert "wears a house, like a monstrous diver's helmet, on his head" (p. 40), but his legs are "banty-bowed and shaky." The dwarf prize fighters in "Box Seat" have "bulging" foreheads: their heads are "huge," but their bodies are foreshortened and deformed.

The unity sought by the human figures that walk the city streets is that between mind and body, spirit and flesh. The enlarged heads and dwarfed bodies signal a norm of fragmentation. Characters are divided in themselves, divided from one another, and divided from the world of natural process.

Occasionally, however, fragmentation is effaced by a sense of union. In the Mammy-Wattah figure described in "Box Seat" there is a mythic force, the antithesis of Rhobert and the dwarfs:

> . . . a portly Negress whose huge rolls of flesh meet about the bones of the seat-arms. A soil-soaked fragrance comes from her. Through the cement floor her strong roots sink down. They spread under the asphalt streets. Dreaming, the streets roll over on their bellies, and suck their glossy health from them. Her strong roots sink down and spread under the river and disappear in blood-lines that waver south. Her roots shoot down. . . . Roots throb. . . . Earth throbs. [p. 62]

In the city, as in the rural South, myth momentarily fuses with dispossession; and poignancy lies in those who attempt to hold this union or to consciously seek it out. This poignancy belongs to John, for example, in "Theater."

As John takes his seat to watch Dorris in dance rehearsal, the "space-dark air grows softly luminous" as "light streaks down upon him from a window high above. One half of his face is orange in it. One half of his face is in shadow. The soft glow of the house rushes to, and compacts about, the shaft of light" (p. 50). John's body is left in darkness, "separate from the thoughts that pack his mind" (p. 50). As he watches Dorris, however, this separation is bridged. Dorris comes "within the footlights' glow" and is momentarily transfigured in the light: "Glorious songs are the muscles of her limbs. And her singing is of canebrake loves and mangroves (pp. 52–53). As John watches, he is "pressed toward a center of physical ecstasy," a union of body with mind, flesh with spirit, Dorris with John, the moment both created and illuminated by the flickering light.

But John seeks to prolong the ectasy intellectually. His mind "sweeps up to follow [the shaft of light]. Mind pulls him upward into dream" (p. 53). The momentary unity is shattered and, as the dance ends, Dorris looks at John: "His whole face is in shadow. She seeks for her dance in it. She finds a dead thing in the shadow which is his dream" (p. 53). In his attempt to fashion, shape, hold, understand the ephemeral vision through making it into "dream," John has lost the moment, traded the dance for a "dead thing."

Throughout *Cane*, time has absolute autonomy. Unlike the mythic cycle of traditional West Africa, it is not subject to human manipulation or redemption. Only occasionally will the continuity of time and spirit come within the human vision; but it is time, not human intention, that determines the flicker. Not entirely dispossessed from time, humanity no longer has control of its possession. Symbolically, throughout *Cane*, the smoke that rises is the smoke of human sacrifice whose efficacy is no longer insurance of the redemption of time.

It is fitting that a work in which time is suspended should end with "Kabnis," for which Toomer has chosen the dramatic form. Prose narrative takes the reader to a point in the past and then forward toward the present, typically presented in past tense; drama takes the audience from the present moment forward into an unknown future. Thematically, in the rejected sacrifice of the Cain-like Kabnis, it is of a piece with the whole. More than that, in the context of the alternation between present and past tense which Toomer makes throughout *Cane*, the implied movement toward the future assumes a specific significance.

Cane begins, in "Karintha," with the present tense of eternal recurrence, much like Armah's descriptions of the sea in *The Beautyful Ones*. The first section of *Cane*, by contrast, ends with a story, "Blood-Burning Moon," narrated in past tense. In between there is an irregular alternation of past and present tense. The second part of *Cane* begins in the present tense; and the final story, "Bona and Paul," is in the present tense until the final two lines: "Paul and the black man shook hands. When he reached the spot where they had been standing, Bona was gone" (p. 78). In these first two portions of *Cane*, beginnings are timeless and endings are timebound, final. But *Cane* represents a suspension rather than a conclusion; and the dramatic form of "Kabnis" is admirably suited to this purpose.

William Attaway, *Blood on the Forge*

Blood on the Forge begins on a Kentucky farm with only "one good strip of land" remaining, farmed by the Moss brothers—Big Mat, Melody, and Chinatown—and Big Mat's barren wife, Hattie. The barrenness of the land and of the woman signal the death of an agrarian and communal way of life. Big Mat's quarrel with a white man only hastens the Moss brothers' departure for the North, and they accept a steel-mill recruiter's offer to board a boxcar for the Allegheny River and a strikebound steel mill there.

Predominantly the narrative focuses on the destructive life in the mill community. The mill workers suffer crippling or fatal accidents: one loses his arm, another his legs (and later his life); Melody damages his hand, and Chinatown loses his eyes; Big Mat is killed in a strike-related riot. The novel concludes with Melody and the blind Chinatown once more on board a train, this time bound for Pittsburgh, using the $250 compensation for Chinatown's eyes to buy their tickets.

The structure and narrative technique of *Blood on the Forge* are largely familiar—the third-person narrator with selective omniscience, the hope for a new and better way of life that meets with disappointment, the destructive cycle in which the present recapitulates the dispossession of the past, and a linear journey that ends where it began. Anna, the prostitute who becomes Mat's woman, has already been discussed as a Mammy-Wattah figure. But there is another facet to Attaway's novel—its jazzlike use of images of fragmentation. These images carry the thematic burden of the novel and provide a solution to the problem of characterization in a novel whose characters are largely inarticulate, incapable of verbal expression.

Melody provides an early clue to this aspect of Attaway's technique. He believes that "a man had oughta know book learnin'—so's he kin know how to say what he's feeling" (p. 27). But earlier he has been described as never having had "a craving in him that he couldn't slick away on his guitar" (p. 1). For Melody, his guitar provides a substitute for words. As the narrative progresses, however, his capacity to give musical shape to his feelings is eroded. Early on, he admits that "every once in a while he would get filled up . . . with a feeling that was too big to turn into any kind of music" (p. 17). Later, in the mill town, his guitar playing changes, from the "slicking" that was "for back home and the distance in the hills" to "quick chords with the finger . . . right for that new place [but] nothin' like the blues that spread fanwise from the banks of the Mississippi," a way of playing better suited to "the whirling lights and . . . the heart of the great red ingots" (p. 33). The stasis of *Cane* gives way to movement, and the images of twilight to images of whirling lights and fragmentation—and this is the change one must imagine in Melody's guitar playing, as he gives voice to his feelings about the milltown and about Anna. His feelings, however, get "too big" for even this changed way of playing; more or less deliberately, he injures his hand and hangs up his guitar. His feelings cut off from their expression, he becomes one of the images of fragmentation in the novel. And it is as though Attaway takes up where Melody leaves off, using a counterpoint of images centering on animals and barrenness that taken together signal that the erosion of time apparent in *Cane* is here complete. In the imagery of fragmentation, time explodes.

In Part I, Mat returns to Mr. Johnston's farm to butcher the pigs he has slaughtered the day before: "The sun was coming up. Nine white carcasses gleamed, gaping open, split down the middle, head and feet gone. They were like nine small human bodies" (p. 30). At the beginning of Part II, the Moss brothers flee Kentucky on the boxcar:

Squatted on the straw-spread floor of a boxcar, bunched up like hogs headed for market, riding in the dark for what might have been years, knowing time only as dippers of warm water gulped whenever they were awake, helpless and drooping because they were headed into the unknown and there was no sun, they forgot even that they had eyes in their heads and crawled around in the boxcar, as though it were a solid thing of blackness. [p. 45]

The metamorphosis of animal to human, human to animal, recurs throughout the novel, along with the notion of slaughter. Time becomes alternately fragmented and opaque, only partially knowable. In the "Mex Town" episode of Part II:

There were dogs everywhere. Stray curs came smelling at [their] heels. They did not kick at them. The whores of Mex Town had more love for animals than for men. One steel worker who had killed a dog had been found on the ash pile. A knife had let his blood soak the ashes. [p. 81]

Later, Chinatown loses his eyes and loses as well even his fragmentary perceptions of time, the red pop and gold teeth that punctuate the darkness. He is looked after by Anna: "Anna would take good care of Chinatown. Like all her kind, she had a ready sympathy for a maimed animal, whether dog or man" (p. 197). In the dogfights that are staged for the workers' amusement and the dog trainer's profit, the description of one man's method of training his dog to fight mimes the "training" Big Mat undergoes for his fight at the conclusion of Part IV:

Son's [the dog's] owner . . . knew how to keep a dog savage and ready for blood. [He] kept Son in a dark closet for weeks at a time, feeding him raw meat sprinkled with gunpowder. Sometimes [he] would let him out and tease him with a sharp stick. Son would tear up anything that came within the radius of his chain. [p. 110]

By the time Big Mat is "deputized" to help control the strikers, he too is "savage" and "ready for blood"—and for much the same reason. He has been locked in darkness: on the boxcar, in a town where days pass with the sun concealed behind steel-mill smoke, and in a work schedule that means rising before dawn and returning from work after dark. Tormented by his growing impotence with Anna, he spends hours of his "free" time balancing a rock at the end of his outstretched arm as a proof of his strength. Chained by the circumstances of his life, Big Mat is more than ready "to tear up anything."

The men's dismemberment in work accidents again mimes the slaughter of the hogs. In the women, too, there is dismemberment and the stench of death: one of the first women the brothers encounter is a black whore with "a rot stink." They are told that "her left breast 'bout rotted off. . . . You kin smell it a mile away" (p. 58).

Images of barrenness figure as another form of fragmentation, of human beings cut off from time and cyclic continuity. In Part I, most of Mat's farmland is so lacking in topsoil that it is barren; and he has no mule for plowing. His wife, Hattie, is barren, having suffered six or seven miscarriages. Though Anna finds in Big Mat a fulfillment of her yearning for a man "with a pine tree on his belly, hard like rock all night" (p. 89), by the end of Part IV she has turned to "a piece of ice" beneath him, "a dead body" (p. 182), and the image again is one of barrenness. Earlier, Mat has explained his barrenness as the result of a curse by God on "a child of sin." He knows how to lift the curse: "I got to preach the gospel—that the only way" (p. 29). But his knowledge, too, is barren: "No matter how much inside [him]," he can't preach. "If I tries to preach 'fore folks it all jest hits against the stopper in my throat and build up and build up till I fit to bust with wild words that ain't comin' out" (p. 29). He lacks the words to bring forth the Word, and belief is fragmented from its expression.

These various images of fragmentation are epitomized in the character of Smothers, the mad, crippled timekeeper at the mill. Smothers feels that the earth will sooner or later take revenge against the steel mill's violation of its sacredness, and the revenge will focus on the men who work the mill. "Steel gonna git you," he says. Crippled in an accident that he brought on himself as an act of defiance of the "monster" mill, he has become a kind of mill worker everyman, his crippled legs his wounds in an ongoing battle. Before he is killed, in the same explosion that takes Chinatown's eyes, his foreman has jokingly promised him that if steel "gits" him, "we make you up into watch fobs. The boys 'round the bunkhouse 'll wear you across their chests for luck" (p. 172). After Smothers's death, Melody passes through the bunkhouse and finds Bo keeping the promise, affixing watch chains to shreds of steel from the explosion.

Smothers's vision and death echo Sekoni's in *The Interpreters*: both are struck down when natural process goes out of control. The Keeper of Time is fragmented into shards, and time explodes.

Ayi Kwei Armah, *Why Are We So Blest?*

Armah's third novel moves from the isolated vision of the man in *The Beautyful Ones* or the portrayal of fragmentation and loss in *Fragments* to the relationship of three individuals to a revolution in progress in an unspecified Portuguese colony in Africa, identified as "Congheria," in its description very much like Guinea-Bissau on the northern Guinea Coast of West Africa. But in *Why Are We So Blest?* the attempt at action proves as impotent as vision does in Armah's other novels. None of the three figures succeeds in actually taking part in the revolution and each is shown as unable to overcome the destructive isolation of his own psyche.

Solo Nkonam, a translator for an Algerian magazine, looks back on his past participation in revolution with disillusionment. Modin Dofu, a Ghanaian student, and Aimée Reitsch, a neurotic American girl, fail in their attempt to join the revolutionaries. The story is a narrative of political failure and political failure manifests a larger, spiritual failure, their distance from the revolution reflecting their spiritual isolation and their imprisonment in self. In the world of *Why Are We So Blest?*, as in the traditional ideal community, this isolation in self is equivalent to spiritual death. Both Solo's names signal this isolation; his surname, loosely translated from Akan, means "lonely stranger." There is irony too in the names Modin Dofu (in Akan,

"I am called a person who loves") and Aimée ("one who is loved"); in the symbolic interplay of isolation and sexuality that structures the novel, love breeds only destruction.

Solo narrates the story, largely on the basis of the notebooks kept by Aimée and Modin, which have come into his hands. A passage from the first entry in Modin's notebook fuses the narrative interplay of sexuality and isolation. The passage deals with Earl Lynch, who "in 25 years might be the first black professor at Harvard." Lynch uses sex as a means of racial retaliation, and makes a point of having affairs with as many of his white colleagues' wives as he can. His use of sex is also an attempt to break out of his own imprisonment in self, an imprisonment that is imaged in Modin's description of Lynch's "secret library." Lynch shares his secret with Modin, who learns that the library is comprised of "standard reading" on Marxism, available "at any book shop." But above the bookshelves, dominating the room, hangs an African mask, which according to Lynch "doesn't have any meaning":

The design was a mask: a pained, human face, a huge head, huge bulbous, all-seeing eyes, pained, distorted ears open to all possible sounds, superimposed on a shriveled mouth and nostrils cramped with hard control. The limbs—emaciated, reduced to spindly lines—were attached indirectly to the human spiderhead. The design gave the creature no chest, no stomach, no groin. From its existence of pain the faculties lodged in those organs had been subtracted by the carver. There were just eight crawly, elongated little limbs about the spider face. [p. 32]

As described by Modin, the mask has "a powerful meaning," part of which comes from the character of the folklore figure it portrays—Ananse, the cunning spider of countless West African stories. The "wisdom of Ananse" is a misguided, self-centered wisdom that often loses touch with reality. In one story, for example, Ananse decides that he will gather up all the wisdom in the world and store it in a calabash at the top of a tall coconut palm. When he thinks he has it all, he ties the calabash around his neck, allowing it to hang down in front—thus making it impossible for him to climb the coconut palm. Ananse's son, Ntikumah, begins to laugh as he watches his father's struggles, and tells him that he would do better to put his load on his back. Realizing the wisdom of Ntikumah's words, Ananse also realizes that he has failed in his attempt to gather up *all* wisdom. In frustration and anger, he drops the calabash, which shatters, allowing wisdom to spread once again throughout the world.

In *Why Are We So Blest?*, Earl Lynch has his own calabash in his secret library. But in Modin's words, it contains only the wisdom of "the white desert." "Caught in the white net of minds," Lynch ironically seeks a "break for his spirit" in "the whitest of philosophies, Marxism" (p. 163). The web of Ananse becomes a circle of imprisonment rather than reciprocity, and Lynch's attempt to escape has only enmeshed him further.

For Modin, the web itself is a symbol of the choices available to the black intellectual.

Those who stay in the peripheral areas intellectually, emotionally, psychologically, totally, are not lonely. They are in touch with home, not cut off. The price they pay for not being lonely, however, is that they suffer the crudest forms of manipulation, mystification, planned ignorance.

Those who shift from the periphery to the center can hope to escape some of these cruder forms of manipulation. But the price they pay is loneliness, separation from home, the constant necessity to adjust to what is alien, eccentric to the self. [p. 33]

At the center of the web is an insensitive Lynch, who sees no meaning in the mask of Ananse. At the center, too, is Solo. Fully aware of his alienation, he opens his narrative by remarking, "Even before my death I have become a ghost" (p. 11). Modin, whom we see as a younger double of Solo, remarks, "The directions made available to me within this arrangement are all suicidal. I am supposed to get myself destroyed but of my own free-seeming choice. Earl [Lynch] is a suicide" (p. 31). At the center of the web is the spiritual death of Lynch and Solo. Aware of this, Modin seeks to reconnect with the periphery, though from the beginning he sees his choice only as a more meaningful choice of death:

The real question is not whether to commit suicide but how best to invest my inevitable destruction. . . . Outside of investing my death in an ongoing effort to change things as they are, it wouldn't matter much

what kind of death I chose. . . . All existent methods are absurd and
deadly outside of a revolutionary commitment to Africa. [p. 31]

To his credit, Modin is repelled by Lynch's use of sex as a racial weapon. Though he has a series of relationships with white
women, initially at least his purpose is pleasure, and the relationships are portrayed with tenderness. When he becomes aware of
sex as an idea, as a weapon, he is revolted. This and his own
sense of survival combine after he is nearly stabbed to death by a
woman's husband, and he swears off even a tacit involvement in
such a battle. Given this, he begins his relationship with
Aimée—also white, but unmarried—only reluctantly; and when
he realizes that she is fantasizing about him as a black violator of
white purity, he nearly breaks it off. Instead of severing the relationship, however, he converts her—as he sees it—to his own
genuine tenderness.

But the relationship between Modin and Aimée is only pe-
ripherally grounded in psychology. More centrally, it is a symbolic relationship between a destroyer, a Circe of sorts, insensitive to the pain she causes, and a victim who seems to realize
from the beginning that he is fated for destruction. They meet
when Modin, having rejected his white-funded scholarship sti-
pend, takes a job as a paid volunteer in a psychological study of
pain. Aimée has volunteered for the study as well, not for the
money but for the "experience." The experiment in pain is an
obvious foreshadowing of the conclusion of the novel: Aimée's
threshold of pain is extraordinarily high, and the experimenters
leave off increasing the voltage of the shocks they are using for
fear of physiological damage. Modin, by contrast, experiences
pain almost immediately. Aimée's insensitivity here—her desire
in fact to know what the experience of pain is—prophesies the
conclusion when she joins in the sexual torture of Modin that
leads to his death.

Disillusioned with intellectual passivity, Aimée and Modin
both decide to "discontinue their studies"—he at Harvard, she at
Radcliffe—and go to Algeria, where they hope to join forces
with the anti-Portuguese revolutionaries who have their headquarters there. From there, they plan to move on to Congheria
and the revolution itself. The Congherians in Algeria reject the

couple, Aimée because she is white, Modin because he is "too intellectual." But they do this tacitly, stringing the couple along
with a perpetual "Come back in two weeks." Modin and Aimée's
money runs out. Solo invites them to share his apartment.
Months pass. Tired of waiting, the two strike out on their own
for Congheria.

A French motorist who has offered them a ride returns later
with three friends. They beat Modin and rape Aimée, and after
an extended sexual torture in which Aimée—not unwillingly
—participates, they cut off Modin's penis with a piece of thin
wire and leave him to bleed to death as they take Aimée back to a
nearby village. The novel concludes with Aimée's description of
the event:

> They used me to get Modin hard. The wounded man gave a yell of
> pain and pulled hard on the wire. First his friend was surprised, then he
> too pulled. The snapping off of the tip of Modin's prick was slow. I
> thought it would fall just like that, but the wire cut into his flesh and
> then in spite of all that tension nothing seemed to happen. Modin did
> not scream. I was thinking the wire had broken when the tip of his penis
> snapped off and hung by just a bit of skin from the bottom. I gathered
> all my strength and shook myself free of the two men holding me. They
> let me go. They were laughing, all of them.
> Modin started bleeding. The blood curved out in a little stream that
> jerked outward about every second. I reached him and without think-
> ing of what I was doing I kissed him. His blood filled my mouth. I
> wanted him to speak to me. He had groaned a little when I took him
> and kissed him, but he said nothing.
> I asked him, "Do you love me?"
> He didn't answer me. [p. 288]

Modin leaves the center of the web to find a recapitulation of
Ananse's pain, in a movement of fatal circularity. He has written
earlier that when he travels, "it is the past that fills my mind. . . .
It always happens when I travel. . . . As my body is taken forward, my mind becomes hungry for places and the things behind me. . . . Everything comes together rapidly. Every journey
in this way becomes a return, another visit into myself" (p. 75).
The reader is left to imagine Modin's awareness that the end of
his journey was embodied in its beginning, in Ananse's web and
in his meeting with Aimée.

Toni Morrison, *Song of Solomon*

Milkman Dead is the center of *Song of Solomon*, initially at least not its hero but simply the focal point of the conflict that structures the novel. Like Lamming's young man in *In the Castle of My Skin*, he is caught between two conflicting visions of time, Slime's fragmentation offered here by Milkman's father, with Pa's vision of continuity offered by his aunt, Pilate. *Song of Solomon* works toward celebration rather than dispossession, however, toward the dominance of a vision in which past and present—Africa and upper Michigan—are fused in a temporal resonance that shapes the novel into the song of a heritage. Conflict, characterization, and narrative structure are all clarified in the light of this temporal resonance, which becomes apparent to the reader only gradually but is implicit in the novel's opening scene.

The novel opens with Robert Smith, a life-insurance agent, perched atop Mercy Hospital, outfitted with blue plastic wings, about to "fly" across Lake Superior. Twenty years and some hundred pages later, Guitar Bains has learned that Smith was a member of the Seven Days, a Mau-Mau-like black organization that has vowed murder for murder, white for black, whose members voluntarily choose suicide when they feel that they might crack emotionally or be found out. Smith has added the accoutrements of madness to his death in order to prevent investigation, thus ensuring the safety of the organization. Symbolically at least, Smith is an extraordinary "life-insurance" agent.

At first, however, the significance of this opening scene remains opaque, and the reader mistakenly takes it for the promise of a novel in which the bizarre must be accepted as commonplace. Placed later in the novel, after the reader has gained a certain familiarity with Morrison's narrative technique, Smith's act would arouse suspicions. Placed as it is, however, the scene seems to signal a world in which madness is the order of the day, a judgment reinforced by the confusion that prevails among the hospital employees and by the strange aspect of the onlookers—among them a well-dressed pregnant woman whose teenage daughters chase red velvet flowers through the snow and a tall woman singing, as though her song, together with the red flowers and the plastic wings, were part of a mad entertainment.

Only when the scene can be placed within the context of the entire narrative does its true significance emerge—a significance that includes Guitar Bains's discovery of the reason for Smith's suicide and the significance of the song that the tall woman, Pilate Dead, sings:

> Sugarman done fly
> Sugarman done gone
> Sugarman cut across the sky
> Sugarman gone home.

At the time it is sung, its words reinforce the apparent madness of the circuslike scene: the onlookers, in fact, listen "as though it were the helpful and defining piano music in a silent movie" (p. 6). By the end of the novel, however, enough information has been offered to assess the song's true significance. It is a song that is sung by the children in Shalimar (pronounced "Shaleemon"), Virginia, to commemorate one of their ancestors, Solomon (also pronounced "Shaleemon"), after whom the town is named. According to local legend, Solomon was a "flying" African slave who "just stood up in the fields one day, ran up some hill, spun around a couple of times, and was lifted up in the air.

Went right on back to wherever it was he came from" (p. 325). The song and the legend allude to a belief among certain slaves, especially perhaps those of Ibo origin, that after death one's spirit would return to the home of the ancestors, a belief that to some extent encouraged suicide among Ibo slaves.

As Milkman will discover, the Solomon/Sugarman of the song is Pilate's own grandfather, Milkman's great-grandfather, the Dead family having originally hailed from Shalimar, Virginia.

In singing "Sugarman" instead of "Solomon" or "Shaleemon," Pilate seems simply to be using a common blues term, but this alteration prophesies a recurrent image pattern of the novel, the association of sweetness with death. Guitar makes the connection explicit when he explains to Milkman sometime later that he cannot eat candy because, after his father was literally sliced into two in a mill accident, his mother bought "divinity" candy (surely an intentional irony on Morrison's part) with a portion of the forty dollars compensation money; and thus for Guitar death is irrevocably linked with the sweet taste of candy. Much later in the novel, a sweet-ginger-like scent in the air is the narrative signal that Milkman is in the present of the dead—when he breaks into Pilate's house to steal the green sack that contains her "inheritance" (her father's bones, which Milkman believes to be gold nuggets); when he visits Circe, the midwife who delivered both his father and Pilate, who by the time of Milkman's visit is clearly one of the ghosts in the novel; and when, at the very end of the narrative, Milkman and Pilate bury her father's bones near Solomon's Leap in Virginia. (The conjunction of a sweet, spicy scent with the spirits of the dead is also an aspect of black folk belief.) The association between sweetness and death is implicit, too, in the name of the young Virginia woman—Sweet —with whom Milkman dallies while his cousin-mistress, Hagar, dies back in Michigan, "lifed" by love, and while Guitar Bains lurks in Virginia shadows, seeking to kill Milkman himself.

Solomon's flight, commemorated in the song, and Smith's flight are part of another pattern of the novel's imagery in which flight is associated with a spiritual triumph and the redemption of time into a sacred continuum. Pilate's spiritual strength is measured by Milkman's comment that "without ever leaving the ground, she could fly" (p. 340), and the strength of Milkman's own vision is emphasized in the concluding sentence of the novel: "For now he knew what Shalimar knew: If you surrendered to the air, you could ride it" (p. 341). In the context of this imagery, the incapacity for flight signals a material oppression of the spirit, a significance that is underscored in an exchange between Guitar Bains and Milkman midway through the novel: somewhat anomalously, a white peacock appears on a blue Buick in a used-car lot near where the two men are conversing, and Guitar explains to Milkman that a peacock cannot fly because "all that jewelry weighs it down. . . . Can't nobody fly with all that shit" (pp. 179–80). Earlier, Milkman's father has used the peacock image to describe the gold nuggets that he thinks he saw as a seventeen-year-old in a Pennsylvania cave (the same nuggets supposed to be Pilate's "inheritance"): "Life, safety, and luxury fanned out before him like the tailspread of the peacock." It is within this pattern of flight versus flightlessness, the transcendence of the spirit versus the oppression of the material, that Milkman journeys toward a spiritual strength of vision.

By the conclusion, the reader can comprehend the resonance of its opening scene, a scene whose seeming madness embodies a palimpsest of meaning in which the linear sequence of the ensuing narrative is first offered as a simultaneous whole. The ghosts, deaths, peacocks, lovers, flights, gold nuggets, and sweet scents and tastes that comprise the narrative substance of *Song of Solomon* are all implicit in the circuslike opening scene. Implicit, too, though again only in retrospect, is the resolution of life-insurance agent Smith's double-consciousness, in which his inner reality and the reader's and onlookers' initial perception of him are redeemed into a unity of self and action. The upshot of Morrison's narrative technique, which requires that the reader weave the pieces into a whole, is that the temporal chaos of No Man's Land is redeemed into a mythic continuum of time and identity, a narrative technique that renders the invisible continuum of time visible to the reader, allowing him to "see" time as clearly as Milkman sees the midwife's ghost and Pilate sees the ghost of her own father. The opening scene of *Song of Solomon*, the moment of Smith's flight, resonates with a cultural and personal past and with the vision the as-yet-unborn Milkman Dead will attain before he in turn dies.

It is within this context of temporal resonance that the conflict centering on Milkman is most clearly illuminated. On the one hand is Milkman's father, Macon Dead, a self-made man, tenement owner in the Michigan city in which most of the novel is set, and husband to the daughter of the city's only black doctor. For Macon Dead, time is money, and the answer to temporal dispossession is the dispossession of others: he literally evicts Guitar Bains's penniless grandmother, and tells Milkman to "own things. Then you'll own yourself and other people too" (p. 55). Like Lamming's Slime, he holds a philosophy equivalent to spiritual death: "Owning, building, acquiring—that was his life, his future, his present, and all the history he knew" (p. 304).

On the other hand is Pilate Dead, Macon's sister, a bootlegger of wine who lives in a house without gas or electricity, who hand pumps her water from a well, and who thinks "progress [is] a word that meant walking a little farther on down the road" (p. 27). Pilate's difference from other people begins with the fact that she "borned herself": after her mother's heart stopped in childbirth, Pilate just "popped out," though the midwife was certain both she and her mother were dead (p. 246). The suggestion that Pilate is self-generated is strengthened by the fact that Pilate's navel falls off along with the umbilical cord shortly after her birth. As an adult, she is "isolated" by this difference: men freeze at the sight of "that belly that looked like a back; became limp even, or cold. . . . women whispered and shoved their children behind them" (p. 149), seeing Pilate as a Conjure Woman whose footprints must be swept up if her powers of evil are to be warded off. As a consequence of this isolation and rejection, Pilate becomes what her strange birth and navelless stomach suggest she is—a self-made person, whose richness, unlike her brother Macon's, is spiritual: she becomes a "healer" with "an alien's compassion for troubled people" (p. 150). Cut off from the living, she has a quiet intimacy with the dead, especially her father, who is both her "mentor" and a source of comfort. Though Pilate saw him shot—"blown five feet in the air"—and buried, she asserts that he is not dead, that a person dies only when he wants to. In contrast to Macon's repudiation of "the past, present and future," Pilate carries her past with her, literally as well as symbolically. From each of the many places she traveled during her youth and young womanhood she collected a stone for remembrance and, at her father's direction, returns to a Pennsylvania cave to collect a sack of bones—of a white man her brother killed, she thinks, but actually those of her own father—which for more than half a century she takes with her wherever she goes.

In sum, Pilate's role in Morrison's mythically conceived novel is that of a traditional Priestess, an intermediary between the spiritual and the material world, a Keeper of Time whose role is as much intuitive as conscious. She cherishes her father's bones without knowing they are his—and at one point lies to the police, telling them the bones are those of her husband, "Mr. Solomon," voicing a mythic truth even when she means to lie. She sings the song of "Sugarman's" flight while Smith is perched atop Mercy Hospital with no conscious knowledge of the song's multiple significance. Named by an illiterate father who chose her name at random from the Bible, Pilate becomes, by way of one of the puns with which the novel abounds, a spiritual "pilot," who need not ask what truth is because, without knowing it, she embodies it, much as she can "fly without ever leaving the ground."

It is between this brother and sister, the repudiator of time and its keeper, that the battle for Milkman's life and soul is waged. Had Macon had his way, Milkman would never have been conceived and, once conceived, never born. Pilate, seeking a reunion with her brother after more than twenty years of separation, arrives in the Michigan city with her daughter Reba and granddaughter Hagar to discover that Macon and his wife, Ruth, have been sexually estranged for more than a decade, Macon having rejected Ruth because (unlike her biblical counterpart) she clings too closely to the memory of her father, leading Macon to suspect her of having committed some unspecified sexual perversity with him. Because Ruth wants another child, Pilate provides her with an aphrodisiac to give Macon; for three days, the two of them are sexually reunited, as a result of which Milkman is conceived. In a rage when he discovers that his wife is pregnant, Macon forces Ruth to try to abort herself with knitting needles and enemas until Ruth, in desperation, once again seeks Pilate's help:

Years later Ruth learned that Pilate put a small doll on Macon's chair in his office. A male doll with a small painted chicken bone stuck between its legs and a round red circle painted on its belly. Macon knocked it out of the chair and with a yardstick pushed it into the bathroom, where he doused it with alcohol and burned it. . . . He left Ruth alone after that. [p. 132]

Milkman is safely born—with a caul which, in the novel as in folk belief, foreshadows his capacity for second sight, a capacity that he shares with his aunt Pilate along with a birth that is as anomalous as hers.

Structurally, in the battle between Macon and Pilate, *Song of Solomon* extends a technique used by Morrison in her two earlier novels, *The Bluest Eye* and *Sula*, both of which are built upon a relationship between two families whose households offer a contrast between order and disorder—in *The Bluest Eye*, the McTeer and Breedlove households; in *Sula*, the Wright (later, Greene) and Peace households. In *Song of Solomon* much the same contrast exists between the two Dead households, the one headed by Milkman's father, the other by his aunt. Throughout the three novels, too, disorder is linked with an openness of sexuality, order with its virtual absence; and in either extreme, there is a potential destructiveness. Disorder may erupt into chaos, as it does in *The Bluest Eye* when Cholly Breedlove rapes and impregnates his eleven-year-old daughter and in *Sula* when Eva Peace intentionally incinerates her son. In *Song of Solomon* Pilate's granddaughter, Hagar, embodies this chaos: in love with Milkman, she would rather kill him than lose him and, failing in that, she dies, "lifed" by love. Conversely, order may collapse into a physical and spiritual barrenness, as happens in the antiseptic Wright household in *Sula* and in Macon Dead's household in *Song of Solomon*.

Beginning with the McTeer sisters' befriending of Pecola Breedlove, however, Morrison's impetus is toward a reconciliation of the two houses, an impetus continued in Nel's friendship with Sula Peace. In these earlier novels, though, the attempt at reconciliation is largely thwarted: Pecola Breedlove, her baby dead, lapses into a madness that is beyond the reach of the McTeer sisters; and after Nel Greene finds her husband and Sula Peace naked in her bedroom, both her marriage and her friendship with Sula are sundered. In *Song of Solomon*, however, the reconciliation is effected by the son of Macon Dead who, by the conclusion of the narrative, has become Pilate's spiritual heir.

In Part II of the novel, thirty-two-year-old Milkman journeys to the distant past—in Pennsylvania, the birthplace of his father and his aunt, and in Virginia, the birthplace of their parents. He is in search of the gold nuggets which, since they are not in Pilate's green sack, must still be in the cave where his father first saw them. What he finds, however, is what he comes to term his "people." In Pennsylvania he finds a community that still remembers his grandfather as the heroic embodiment of their own ideals, a blacksmith who fashioned Pilate's earring in which she keeps the paper on which her father had laboriously printed the name he had chosen from the Bible, and the very tangible ghost of the midwife who delivered both his father and his aunt. In Virginia, he discovers that his great-grandfather, the Solomon of the song, had fathered an entire community before "flying" away. The gold he finds is the richness of a heritage, as he consciously and painstakingly pieces together what Pilate seems intuitively to have known all along—that only in communion with the dead may the Dead come spiritually to life. In the final scene of the novel, he returns to Solomon's Leap with Pilate to bury her father's bones: enveloped in an "odor like crystallized ginger . . . a scent that could have come straight from a marketplace in Accra" (pp. 185–86), Pilate and Milkman bear common witness to a heritage in which West Africa and the antebellum South converge with a 1963 reality in which Martin Luther King declares his dream from the foot of the Lincoln Memorial and ninety-three-year-old W. E. B. DuBois dies on the outskirts of Accra, in Christiansborg Castle (whence the reader may imagine the Solomon of Morrison's novel to have originally come). Pilate dies, Milkman is on the point of death; but by this moment in the mythic contour of Morrison's narrative, the reader has learned that life has very little to do with the body and a good deal to do with the spirit. One is left believing that the common reality which Pilate and Milkman embody continues: *Song of Solomon* is the voice of that reality.

Early in the novel, Milkman learns from his father how his grandfather got the name of Macon Dead. A drunken Yankee soldier confused the information to be put on his freedmen's papers: "He asked Papa where he was born. Papa said Macon. Then he asked him who his father was. Papa said, 'He's dead.' Asked him who owned him, Papa said, 'I'm free.' Well the Yankee wrote it all down, but in the wrong spaces. Had him born in Dunfrie, . . . and in the space for his name the fool wrote, Dead comma Macon" (p. 53). Seemingly, however, it is not only the Yankee who was confused: all other indications in the novel have Milkman's grandfather born in Shalimar, Virginia, not Macon. Nowhere in the narrative is this discrepancy resolved, but one may conjecture a number of possibilities. First, Milkman's father may simply have got the story wrong. Second, Morrison may obliquely be underscoring a fact of black history, an absence of reliable birth records that in many instances makes it impossible to ascertain a family's history. The discrepancy takes on a clearer significance in the context of the other anomalous births in the novel, specifically Pilate's and Milkman's —both born against all odds, their survival a credit to their spiritual strength. In this light, it becomes possible, symbolically at least, that their common ancestor was born simultaneously in two different places, possessed of a mythic power that countered the rational impossibility of such a birth. Thus, Pilate and Milkman are symbolically the heirs of a multiple lineage. Outlandish as it may seem, this third conjecture is given a certain credence when one explores the significance of the novel's title.

Morrison's novel, of course, takes its title from the biblical "Song of Solomon," and the female members of the Dead family—Pilate, Reba (Rebecca), Hagar, Ruth, and Milkman's two older sisters, First Corinthians and Magdalena—have biblical names. The significance of these biblical allusions is more ironic

than straightforward: Ruth clings to her father's memory, not
her husband's; Pilate, in contrast to the New Testament figure,
knows the truth, and her name is a pun; Hagar dies childless.
But the biblical "Song of Solomon" portrays a ritual marriage, symbolically that of Christ to the Church. In Morrison's
novel, there is a similar marriage—the union of Milkman Dead
with his heritage which, like Christ's marriage to the Church, redeems time into an eternal continuum. And there is a second allusion implied in Morrison's title.

In *The Souls of Black Folk*, W. E. B. DuBois takes his epigraph
for a chapter entitled "The Black Belt" from the biblical song:

> I am black, but comely, O ye daughters of Jerusalem,
> As the tents of Kedar, as the curtains of Solomon.
> Look not upon me, because I am black,
> Because the sun hath looked upon me:
> My mother's children were angry with me;
> They made me the keeper of the vineyards;
> But mine own vineyard have I not kept.

Like DuBois, Morrison echoes both the comeliness and the sorrow implicit in the biblical description of the black woman; and
in this sense both writers are most appropriately seen as drawing
on a common source. But Morrison also seems to be echoing
DuBois directly, alluding to the substance of "The Black Belt" itself. DuBois's chapter begins: "Out of the North the train thun-
dered, and we woke to see the crimson of Georgia" (p. 285), and
goes on to chronicle the poverty and debt that characterized the
lives of the million black people in Georgia at the turn of the
century, specifically that part of Georgia "below Macon [where]
the world grows darker; for now we approach the Black
Belt,—that strange land of shadows, at which even slaves paled
in the past, and whence come now only faint and half-intelligible
murmurs to the world beyond" (pp. 286–87). In Morrison's *Song
of Solomon*, the first Macon Dead grows Georgia peaches on his
Pennsylvania farm; Pilate, in upper Michigan, offers Georgia
peaches to her brother's wife on the two occasions when Ruth
comes to her in distress. The Dead family finds both pride and
comfort in this link with the Black Belt. In a larger sense, *Song of*

Solomon celebrates a heritage that includes all the dispossessed, celebrates a people who have survived DuBois's "strange land of shadows" symbolized by the landscape "below Macon," celebrates those who are in fact the descendants of Macon, giving voice to the "half-intelligible murmurs" and thus redeeming the Macon dead into the continuity of time.

Wole Soyinka, Season of Anomy

In *Season of Anomy* Soyinka portrays a mythical community of Aiyéró as a foil to the anomic "Ilosa" and "Cross-River" countries that are controlled by a cocoa cartel and characterized by brutality and slaughter, a carnage directed specifically toward an unnamed tribal group. Illosa and Cross-River, though undoubtedly universal in their implications, are clearly symbolic of Nigeria, the slaughter reminiscent of the historical events that led up to the Biafran secession and civil war, the unnamed tribal group its Ibo victims. Aiyéró, in contrast to the Illosa and Cross-River areas, is an idyllic community:

> A quaint anomaly, had long governed and policed itself, was so singly-knit that it obtained a tax assessment for the whole populace and paid it before the departure of the pith-helmeted assessor in cash, held all property in common, literally, to the last scrap of thread on the clothing of each citizen—such an anachronism gave much patronising amusement to the cosmopolitans of a profit-hungry society. [p. 2]

During the time of the slave trade, Aiyéró broke off from a parent community, Aiyétómò. Ahime, the Chief Minister, explains that the split was caused by religion: "One day one of our men had this thought. He told himself, we base our lives on the teachings of this white god yet the bearers of that faith kill, burn, maim, loot and enslave our people. It is time, he said, to return to the religion of our fathers" (p. 10). Ahime identifies the religion of the "fathers" only as the "religion of the Grain," but the reader learns later that the community "grants Ogun pride of place," the reason being that he is the god of smithies—the makers of the guns that Aiyéró plans to use "if the slave-raiders come again" (p. 13). In part, the significance of the split with Aiyétómò is revealed in the meanings of their names: Aiyétómò, loosely translated from Yoruba, means "the world of a child"; Aiyéró is "the world where we are." The new name reflects Aiyéró's judgment that it is a childishly self-destructive illusion for a people to seek spiritual sanction in the god of another people who are in the process of destroying them. Aiyéró understands what Ezeulu perceives in *Arrow of God* only at the end—that a god who does not embody the values of a people should be rejected. Aiyéró's secession from Aiyétómò has been an attempt to come to terms with the reality of the world as it is.

The source of Aiyéró's spiritual strength lies in its alliance with the regenerative natural cycle, manifested in the homage it pays to Ogun, but in other ways as well. Its head of state, the Custodian of the Grain, symbolizes this alliance. There is a half-comic suggestion that he fathers all the children in Aiyéró, and in any event he is their ritual father, their link with the spiritual continuum of time. Aiyéró is the site of a model cocoa farm and of a film project on the life cycle of cocoa from "seed to ripening"; but the film extends its focus to include a symbolic parallel of the child "from seed to maturity" (p. 20). The young men who leave Aiyéró for the "neon lights" of Illosa and the Cross-River country are a testament to Aiyéró's appeal: they remain uncorrupted by the city and invariably return after their studies or a period of employment. Ahime is a religious figure as well. Described as a "priest," he is the main character's instructor during his initial stay in the community and is later responsible for the sacrificial killing of the bulls in a funeral ceremony.

In this portrayal of Aiyéró Soyinka offers the traditional African spiritual-political ideal. Survival and spiritual continuity are inextricable. At the same time, the Religion of the Grain is not passive or pacifistic: Ogun is the god of gunmakers. It becomes obvious in *Season of Anomy* that the celebration of the past is not a retreat from political problems, but rather a potential source of strength in political battle.

Ofeyi, the main character, grows in vision during the course of the narrative, recapitulating the history of Aiyéró in its split with Aiyétómò. He begins as a song writer and promotions man for the cocoa cartel whose money stands behind the corrupt governments of Ilosa and the Cross-River country. When he journeys to Aiyéró at the beginning of the novel he is caught up in the idyllic quality of the community and convinces his employers to allow him to start a model cocoa farm to be filmed for advertising. By the conclusion of the narrative, he has identified himself not only with the idyll but with the militant strength within it. He puts the vision he acquires into increasingly militant practice.

First, still an employee of the cartel, he writes promotional songs that are only semidisguised invectives against it. After telling how even the gods came to prefer cocoa to ambrosia and passed on their discovery to mankind, one song continues:

> The sweet-toothed ones alas lacked all moderation
> No man-made laws restrained them
> They milked the cocoa-tree in a mass operation
> They drained the nectar, peeled the gold
> The trees were bled prematurely old
> Nor green nor gold remained for the next generation [p. 35]

The Cartel desecrates nature and abandons any traditional continuity between generations. Its materialistic impetus is familiar, and is directly linked with the disruption of cyclic process. Ofeyi judges the actions of the Cartel in terms of the ideal represented by Aiyéró.

Slightly later, using his promotional tours as a cover, Ofeyi begins to organize the Aiyéróans who work in various communities of Ilosa and the Cross-River country. His dream is to make them a nucleus of a national regeneration according to the values of Aiyéró. One community in particular, a group engaged in building a bridge on the border between Ilosa and Cross-River, has also built a symbolic bridge between their ideals and the natives of the area. The Cartel slowly realizes that Ofeyi is working at odds with Cartel interests. His employers send him on a "study tour" of Europe, where they hope he will realign his values with theirs. On this tour, a brief meeting with two strangers in an airport bar becomes extended into friendship when flights are canceled, and both strangers return to figure in later events of the narrative. "The Dentist" is a political assassin who intends to return home and focus his activities on the corrupt directors of the Cartel and their political cohorts, Taiila an Indian woman who reminds Ofeyi of his fiancée at home. Ofeyi cuts his study tour short, returns home, and is fired.

The Cartel's dismissal of Ofeyi is only one aspect of a widespread retaliation against the activities of Aiyéróans throughout the country: "The Cartel [has] identified its tormentors and organized a return harassment." Though the people of Aiyéró are prepared for "evictions from their homes, punitive taxation, loss of jobs, even arbitrary detentions and trumped-up charges," the Cartel's retaliation takes on the configuration of what Ahime describes as a "holocaust" whose dimensions later will include mass murder and torture, particularly in the Muslim-dominated, Cartel-funded Cross-River country. Ofeyi becomes involved in the battle there only partly for reasons of principle. There is a more immediate, personal reason: he learns from his friend Zaccheus, a musician in the Cartel's promotional band which Ofeyi formerly directed, that his fiancée, Iriyise, has been kidnaped in the Cross-River country. The remainder of the narrative charts Ofeyi's search for and ultimate rescue of Iriyise from the Cross-River country.

In Aiyéró, Iriyise has undergone her own spiritual transformation. At the beginning of the narrative she has been described as a "gin-drinking goddess of the neon lights of the capital." She is also a member of Ofeyi's promotional troupe, her role being to reenact a mock ritual of rebirth as she emerges from a gigantic cocoa pod:

The mammoth pod split open lengthways, or across its girth, top half opening like a lid. Iriyise rose from a bed of simulated giant beans as from sleep, stretched her arms. The orchestra played and Zaccheus, dressed in tails, handed her a cup of cocoa, bent on one knee and she stepped out on his back. And the multitude of headgears, neither wig nor shrub—Ofeyi called them seasonals—they came in green, gold, brown, amber, cream and blends of other colours. On the better equipped stage, the pod might rise through the door, Iriyise sealed within it. [p. 40]

Under the influence of Aiyéró, the mockery of this hocus-pocus becomes reality, as Iriyise goes to work on the cocoa farm:

In wrapper and sash with the other women of Aiyéró, her bared limbs and shoulders among young shoots, Iriyise weaving fronds for the protection of the young nursery, bringing wine to the sweating men in their struggle against the virgin forests. Again and again Ofeyi allowed himself the pleasures of astonishment at her transformations, her unending capacity to learn. From merely singing praises of the "cocoa complexion" she had burgeoned in unforeseeable directions. Now she could even tell a blight on the young shoot apart from mere scorching by the sun. Her fingers spliced wounded saplings with the ease of a natural healer. Her presence, the women boasted, inspired the rains. [p. 20]

In her alliance with the natural world of fertility and growth, instead of the neon-lit artifice of the Cartel, Iriyise becomes a Priestess, her presence a spiritual force for life.

To this point in the narrative, the Cartel and its hirelings have remained vaguely malevolent background figures. Even the kidnaping of Iriyise occurs offstage, reported secondhand to Ofeyi and to the reader. It is only when Ofeyi and Zaccheus journey to the Cross-River country that they, and the reader, experience the mad brutality of the Cartel's desecration.

Lending Soyinka's narrative credibility at this point is the care he takes to describe the interlinkage of power, particularly in the Cross-River country. The Cartel grows its cocoa in the rain forest regions, including Aiyéró, and makes its money selling cocoa products throughout the loose federation of political units described. The Cross-River country is bushland savannah, and poor. It survives by bartering a share of its political power for a share of the Cartel's money. This political power is shared, as is the Cartel's money, by a dual superstructure, one a traditional emirate, one a civil legacy of colonialism, consisting of soldiers, policemen, civil servants, and politicians. But the depredation is in large part the work of bands of men under the authority of the emir, Zaki Amuri. The civil structure only sometimes collab-

orates with them by willfully ignoring their victimization of
Aiyéróans and their friends. Moreover, the emir has lost control
of his men, and their acts are only partly the manifestation of a
planned retaliation against Aiyéró: their sadistic torture springs
less from political vengeance than from sheer perversion.
Ahime's term "holocaust" is well chosen.

Two incidents that occur before Ofeyi and Zaccheus enter
Cross-River in their search for Iriyise foreshadow what they will
find there. Ofeyi, watching a parade of soldiers, remembers a
newspaper photograph:

[a] woman dead of machine-gun bullets, whose hand still tightly
clutched an infant's legs. The infant's head was a pulp of brain and
bone. Did madness enter her with that same bullet which first passed
through the child that was feeding at her breast? The breast hung free
and her milk had mingled in blood to paint a testament of damnation
on earth, beside spilled peppers, an upturned stool and a bowl of pap.
[p. 141]

This episode and an event that occurs later as Ofeyi and
Zaccheus drive down the road to Cross-River demonstrate the
gratuitous horror of the chaos, directed not just at killing bodies
but at the destruction of the procreative cycle itself. In the later
episode, Ofeyi is driving fast and swerves to avoid what seems to
be a monkey dashing across the road in front of his car. He stops
some distance down the road and realizes it is a man pursued by
hunters with bows and arrows.

Then someone unsheathed a dagger. . . . It rose, glinted briefly in the
sun and the old man stooped and drew it across the throat of the pros-
trate figure. His hand moved again, this time down the body, the knife-
tip drew a swift, practised circle on the crotch and his other hand held
up the victim's genitals. He passed it to one of the many eager hands
which also uselessly held open a jaw that had opened wide to thrust out
pain. Into that mouth they stuffed his penis with the testicles. Then
they all stepped back and looked on the transformation they had
wrought. Their faces betrayed neither thought nor feeling. [p. 174]

Some thirty miles later, the two men drive across Labbe Bridge,
"the formal doorway to the territory of hell." But the reader
realizes, as they do, that "it was a purely formal doorway; the

terror had spilled over to outlying villages below the bridge as they had only too grimly discovered on the way" (p. 192).

This hell is dominated by the destruction specifically directed against religion and the land itself. On a peaceful Sunday morning, Zaccheus and Ofeyi lie on the hills above the town of Kuntua and "survey the alien [Aiyéróan] quarters with binoculars" (p. 196). They see white-robed men bar the doors and seal the windows of a church full of worshipers and set it on fire. As the congregation breaks through the barricades, the terrorists kill them with spears and arrows and mutilate their bodies. One woman is "nearly overbalanced by the heavy pregnancy that stuck out of her and seemed ready to weigh her to the ground. . . . Her head jerked suddenly downwards to stare in surprise at the unnatural blossom that her womb had sprouted" (p. 201). There are other horrors: a deserted, half-completed dam filled with "floating bodies so still that they seemed anchored . . . a wax work display of shapes" (p. 171), small children hurled from trains, and other corpses left to pollute rivers and streams.

It is against the mythic dimension of this catastrophe that the success of Ofeyi's mission must be measured. He is not alone in his battle. In one of his attempts to locate Iriyise, he has been directed to a hideout of Aiyéróans waiting to journey back to Aiyéró and to safety—a group whose leader is Ahime, come to help in the rescue of his people. Ofeyi learns for the first time that "the Dentist" carries out his assassinations under the aegis of Aiyéró and is helping Ahime in the rescue mission. Later, Ofeyi goes to a hospital morgue, looking for Iriyise, who may be dead. There he encounters an Indian doctor, Ramath, who has been at work for weeks with little sleep, attempting to heal the victims of the holocaust. Ramath invites Ofeyi to his home for dinner, where Ofeyi discovers Taiila, the Indian woman whom he had met in Europe—the doctor's sister. In the peace of Ramath's home, Ofeyi finds a "microcosm of Aiyéró" (p. 238). Taiila's quest for inner peace has led her to the Cross-River hell, where it has become, like Ofeyi's quest, militant as well as spiritual, as she shelters Aiyéróan victims and aids her brother in his work. The Ramaths' neighbor is "Semi-dozen," a congenial Aiyéróan who has acquired his name from his habit of downing half a dozen bottles of stout each evening. Semi-dozen's family has been massacred, and he has taken explosives from the mine where he works and is waiting for the Cross-River natives to come to him, planning to blow them up when they do, along with himself. Ofeyi, Zaccheus, and the doctor help him to escape his predators, who remain within the house as it explodes.

Ofeyi's encounters with the various people who share his vision of the ideal manifest the sense of community that many characters in black fiction lack. Ofeyi is not alone but part of a diverse group of people who share his celebration of Aiyéróan ideals.

A symbolic tour de force concludes the novel. Ofeyi has reason to believe that Iriyise has been confined to the Temoko prison, which is under the supervision of a clubfooted man named Karaun. The prison is cut off almost entirely from the outside world by concrete walls and the absence of working telephones. It is, nevertheless, a symbolic microcosm of the larger world. Karaun acknowledges that he has Iriyise and agrees to lead Ofeyi to her. As they pass through the inner recesses of the prison,

. . . one fenced-in yard led to another. A chamber of horrors revealed its nature slowly, without warning. . . . Ofeyi found himself face to face—a mere few yards between himself and the nearest of them—with a scattering of inmates who struck him instantly as being—this was his first definition—incomplete. A wide-sweeping glance described a canvas of missing parts; a moment later he realized that he was in a yard of lepers." [p. 294]

Karaun explains that they keep the prisoners awaiting death in a yard beyond the lepers: "Our people have such a horror of lepers that . . . it is the best form of security" (p. 295). The lepers, as physically incomplete as those outside Temoko prison are spiritually crippled, reenact in a quarrel over food the insanity that Ofeyi has seen in Cross-River. Once the quarrel starts, it spreads into a riot in which the original cause has been forgotten: "Bowls, crutches, spoons and checker boards flew across the yard. Doors were rattled open, slammed, the dust bins set up a din and improvised missiles flew across the fence in every direction" (p. 301). A gigantic mute, the prisoner Subaru—who has become Karaun's "right-hand man"—pours buckets of cold water over the rioting lepers. Passing on through the death cells with his deformed guide, Ofeyi enters the lunatic yard, realizes that this is where Karaun has put Iriyise, and grabs Karaun in outrage. The leper riot has spread to the lunatic yard. Just as Subaru knocks him unconscious, Iriyise's limp body lands at Ofeyi's feet.

The world portrayed in this passage to the center of the prison is one where the keepers and the prisoners are interchangeable, as is also indicated by the song the workers sing outside Karaun's window as Ofeyi is waiting: "and you keeper, and me prisoner both are one and the same" (p. 293). And the walls that surround Temoko prison, like the river one must cross to enter Cross-River, are no barricade either to keep the evil in or to keep it out. Similarly, Cross-River becomes a microcosm of the universe at large, and Aiyéró's name, "the world where we are," takes on an aspect of universal symbolism: Aiyéró must make its affirmation in the midst of the madness and defy the collaboration between keepers and prisoners, predators and victims, that occurs both inside and outside of Temoko prison. The meaning of the Aiyéróan ideal depends on its willing confrontation of evil: as Ahime outlines to Ofeyi his plans to lead the Aiyéróans back to Aiyéró, he also notes that this journey back to their spiritual source only marks "the route for a more determined return" (p. 218). The ultimate success of Ofeyi's mission in Temoko prison becomes symbolic of the triumph of the Aiyéróan ideal over the forces of evil.

In the final episode of the novel, Ofeyi confronts this evil and converts it into good. He awakens with a sore head, lying on the ground next to the cot where a comatose Iriyise lies. As he attempts to revive her, Subaru enters with water. In his despair, Ofeyi shouts at Subaru: "I would like to ask you why I am trapped in this place. . . . And this woman is here who should be in hospital, receiving specialized care. Does it not seem strange to you my friend? Or do you see it all as part of ordinary, normal existence I wonder? But you stay dumb. If you could pretend to be deaf I expect you would" (p. 314). Unexpectedly, Subaru pulls "from some inner pocket of his uniform a poster of Iriyise emerging from a neatly cracked gold egg-shape that represented the pod." He then mimes an answer to Ofeyi's question: "The woman's condition was like that egg and Ofeyi must wait, patiently, for her emergence" (p. 314). Ofeyi, seeing that Subaru is not the brute that he had imagined but "a man of images," returns to him his own comparison:

> "Why can't you see that you've been trapped like her in a capsule of death? The milk rots in the coconut if left too long. The child rots in the womb if it exceeds nine months, or else it emerges a monster. . . . Can't I reach you in your coffin where you have been forced to lie these twenty years of your short life? . . . Goodnight then. But for faithful dogs like you the Amuris of this world could not trample down humanity with such insolence. You snap at the heels of those who would confront them and afterwards you bury their bones in the back garden. But remember this Subaru . . . ," he turned and faced him again, holding the trusty's eyes in his, "only you can sniff out the spot and root out the bones to accuse them. After the licks and the caresses, don't complain if the Amuris finally throw you a poisoned bone. Sleep well my friend" [pp. 315–16]

Zaccheus, the Indian doctor, and the Dentist contrive to enter the prison by bribing the guards, and rescue Ofeyi and Iriyise. As Subaru follows their directives, he seems only to be following the bribed Karaun's orders; but when they reach the prison gate, Subaru locks it behind them and accompanies all but the doctor as they join the larger group of Aiyéróans on their way back to Aiyéró. The book ends with the sentence, "In the forests, life began to stir" (p. 320).

The Priestess of cyclic renewal has been rescued, and one of her captors is converted. The celebration of myth, a strong sense of community, and an armed willingness to annihilate history have redeemed the Priestess and have redeemed time. The evil remains, but the source of good is once again in the hands of Aiyéró, her promised rebirth a prophecy of spiritual renewal not in isolation, but in the world. No Man's Land will be redeemed into the goodness of time.

The power of Soyinka's myth derives from a specifically African circumstance and the affirmation of a traditional African concept of the sacred continuum. Simultaneously, however, Soyinka echoes the Western myth of Orpheus. Ofeyi, the musician, rescues his wife after crossing a river to the underworld of Cross-River, clearly divided into an outer Erebus and the Tartarus of the inner prison. He is guided toward the inner recesses of the prison by a deformed Charon-like guide who demands more than pennies for his pay. The prison is guarded by a mute who is consistently described in images of a monstrous Cerberus-like dog. Strengthening this parallel is the Yoruba echo of the names of these characters' Greek counterparts. Orpheus becomes Ofeyi (Ó-fay-ee, stress on the first syllable); Eurydice becomes Iriyise (i-RÍ-yee-shee). Charon becomes Karaun (KÁ-rawn), and Cerberus Subaru (SUÉ-buh-ru).

It is insufficient to note that Soyinka has Africanized a motif of Western literature. In a narrative that equates evil with the influence of the West, Soyinka's African analogue of a Western myth is used as a weapon, one that has been symbolically seized from the intruders and used against them. To see the analogue without simultaneously perceiving this irony is to falsify Soyinka's achievement.

Epilogue

Beyond "Divers Schedules"

Olivia. I will give out divers schedules of my beauty: it shall be inventoried, and every particle and utensil labelled to my will: as Item, Two lips, indifferent red; Item, two grey eyes, with lids to them; Item, One neck, one chin, and so forth.

Twelfth Night, I. 5

In defense of his somewhat narrow focus, one critic of black literature cites the fable about the blind men and the elephant: one critic may emphasize one aspect, another critic something else, but they all contribute to our understanding of the elephant's configuration. His assumption is that one day we may find a sufficient number of blind men to chart the entire animal.

He is misguided, I think. One version of the fable about the blind men and the elephant ends with all the blind men dead, the victims of one another's (or perhaps the elephant's) fury. Some might applaud the possibility, but I for one am worried about the fate of the elephant: at a certain point in the analysis of any phenomenon, including literature, "divers schedules" in themselves cease to be very meaningful. For black fiction, I believe that point has come.

Hitherto, the analysis of black fiction has been characterized by fragmentation, both geographic and ideological in nature. For the most part, attention has been confined to Africa *or* the United States *or* the

Caribbean.[1] Moreover, critics have tended to polarize into two ideological camps. One camp emphasizes the primacy of the message, the substance, of black literature, asserting that "form and structure [are] little more than cousins to content."[2] The other camp stresses the importance of form: "The color line exists not between the covers of a book but outside, in the real world. . . . It is the art, in the long run, that matters."[3] A good deal of energy has been devoted to this argument, often with the consequence that the literature itself has been reduced to the status of a weapon in an ongoing battle.[4] At the least, the intent of the preceding chapters has been to see black fiction whole, as a phenomenon that transcends geographic and national boundaries and in which structure is inseparable from substance. I believe that in various ways the focus on time has served this intention well.

First, it has demonstrated a continuity of vision among a diversity of black writers—African, Caribbean, American, men and women from the late nineteenth-century to the present. There are differences among them as well, to be sure, but their shared use of time in characterization, theme, and narrative structure indicates a unity that lies beyond individual variation. Second, it has clarified certain differences between black and Western fiction, significant enough to suggest that in some in-

1. For example, Eustace Palmer, *Introduction to the African Novel* (New York: Africana, 1972); Robert Bone, *The Negro Novel in America* (New Haven: Yale University Press, 1958); and Kenneth Ramchand, *The West Indian Novel and Its Background* (New York: Barnes and Noble, 1970).
2. Addison Gayle, *The Way of the New World* (New York: Doubleday, 1975), p. xx.
3. Bone, p. 246; p. 7.
4. Summary accounts of this battle recur in studies of black fiction. Bone provides one, with a conclusion that is appropriate to his primacy-of-art point of view. Palmer does much the same thing in his book on the African novel, also arguing for the primacy of form. Gayle, taking the stance that the message is primary, includes such a summary. For a discussion of the pitfalls of such an argument as it relates specifically to African literature, see Bonnie Jo Barthold, "Three West African Novelists: Chinua Achebe, Wole Soyinka, and Ayi Kwei Armah," Ph.D. Dissertation, University of Arizona, 1975.

stances viewing black fiction through the lens of Western literary conventions distorts and diminishes the achievement of the black writer.

Third, the focus on time in large part reconciles the conflict between those who would emphasize the primacy of form and those who stress content and social relevance. Since time in the hands of the black writer is inseparable from both, content is clarified rather than obscured by an attention to form; and form assumes the potential of being revolutionary.

Finally, and more theoretically, time in black fiction is a point where imagination and reality intersect. In traditional Africa, cyclic time had the status of a mythic absolute, and reality was shaped to its configuration: Okonkwo's heroism, for example, recapitulates the heroism of Umuofia's founder. Consistently, however, the myth is brought into question. Time in black fiction becomes not a myth but a "fiction"—responsive to, "pressured" by reality.[5] Time, for example, can die. Even the traditional society is portrayed so that time becomes contingent as Okonkwo, for example, becomes estranged from it. In the imagined past is the reality of the present. In the celebration of cyclic time is the knowledge of its erosion.

In sum, the focus on time avoids the fragmentation that has characterized the criticism of black fiction. And by avoiding this fragmentation, it has illuminated rather than diminished the richness of black fiction.

5. I am using the terms "fiction" and "pressured" here as Wallace Stevens does in "The Noble Rider and the Sound of Words," *The Necessary Angel* (New York: Random House, 1958). Stevens's point is that, although the poet's task is to remake reality, he is nevertheless answerable to its pressures: he cannot escape into a world of past myth.

Works Cited

Abraham, Willie. *The Mind of Africa*. Chicago: Univ. of Chicago Press, 1962.

Achebe, Chinua. *Arrow of God*. London: Heinemann, 1964.

———. *No Longer at Ease*. London: Heinemann, 1960.

———. *A Man of the People*. New York: John Day, 1966.

———. *Things Fall Apart*. London: Heinemann, 1958.

Armah, Ayi Kwei. *The Beautyful Ones Are Not Yet Born*. Boston: Houghton-Mifflin, 1968.

———. *Fragments*. Boston: Houghton-Mifflin, 1970.

———. *Two Thousand Seasons*. Nairobi: E. African Publishing House, 1973.

———. *Why Are We So Blest?* New York: Doubleday, 1972.

Attaway, William. *Blood on the Forge*. New York: Doubleday, 1941.

Baldwin, James. *Another Country*. New York: Dial, 1962.

———. *Go Tell It on the Mountain*. New York: Dell, 1965.

———. *If Beale Street Could Talk*. New York: Dial, 1974.

Baldwin, James and Margaret Mead. *A Rap on Race*. Philadelphia: Lippincott, 1971.

Barthold, Bonnie Jo. "Three West African Novelists: Chinua Achebe, Wole Soyinka, and Ayi Kwei Armah." Ph.D. Dissertation, University of Arizona, 1975.

Blassingame, John. *The Slave Community: Plantation Life in the Ante-Bellum South*. New York: Oxford Univ. Press, 1972.

Bone, Robert. *The Negro Novel in America*. New Haven: Yale Univ. Press, 1965.

Chase, Richard. *The American Novel and Its Tradition*. Garden City, N.Y.: Doubleday, 1957.

Chesnutt, Charles. *The Conjure Woman*. Ann Arbor: Univ. of Michigan Press, 1969.

———. *The House Behind the Cedars*. Boston and New York: Houghton-Mifflin, 1961.

Christensen, James. "The Adaptive Functions of the Fanti Priesthood," in *Continuity and Change in African Culture*. Ed. Melville Herskovits and William R. Bascom. Chicago: Univ. of Chicago Press, 1962.

Davidson, Basil. *The African Genius: An Introduction to African Social and Cultural History*. Boston: Little, Brown, 1969.

Demby, William. *Beetlecreek*. New York: Rinehart, 1950.

Doob, Leonard. "The Psychological Pressure upon Modern Africans," in *Modern Africa*. Ed. Peter McEwan and Robert Sutcliffe. New Haven, Yale Univ. Press, 1961.

DuBois, W. E. B. *The Quest of the Silver Fleece*. Chicago: McClurg, 1911.

———. *The Souls of Black Folk*, in *Three Negro Classics*. New York: Avon, 1968.

Ekwensi, Cyprian. *Jagua Nana*. London: Hutchinson, 1961.

Eliade, Mircea. *The Myth of the Eternal Return or, Cosmos and History*. Trans. Willard R. Trask. Princeton: Princeton Univ. Press, 1971.

Ellison, Ralph. *Invisible Man*. New York: New American Library, 1952.

Fanon, Frantz. *The Wretched of the Earth*. New York: Grove, 1968.

Finnegan, Ruth. *Oral Literature in Africa*. Oxford: Clarendon, 1970.

Franklin, John Hope. *From Slavery to Freedom: A History of Negro Americans*. New York: Vintage, 1969.

———. "Introduction" to *Three Negro Classics*. New York: Avon, 1968.

Gaines, Ernest. *The Autobiography of Miss Jane Pittman*. New York: Dial, 1971.

———. *Catherine Carmier*. Chatham, N.J.: Chatham Booksellers, 1972.

———. "A Long Day in November," in *Bloodline*. New York: Dial, 1968.

———. *Of Love and Dust*. New York: Dial, 1967.

Gayle, Addison. *The Way of the New World: The Black Novel in America*. New York: Doubleday, 1975.

Guillen, Claudio, "Second Thoughts on Literary Periods," in *Literature as System*. Princeton: Princeton Univ. Press, 1971.

Herskovits, Melville. *The Myth of the Negro Past*. Boston: Beacon, 1958.

———. "A Preliminary Consideration of the Culture Areas of Africa." *American Anthropologist* (1924), 26: 88–102.

———, and William R. Bascom. "The Problem of Stability and Change in African Culture," in *Continuity and Change in African Culture*. Ed. William R. Bascom and Melville J. Herskovits. Chicago: Univ. of Chicago Press, 1962.

Hurston, Zora Neale. *Jonah's Gourd Vine*. Philadelphia: Lippincott, 1934.

———. *Their Eyes Were Watching God*. Greenwich, Conn.: Fawcett, 1969.

Izevbaye, D. S. "Ayi Kwei Armah and the 'I' of the Beholder," in *A Celebration of Black and African Writing*. Ed. Bruce King and Kolawole Ogungbesan. New York: Oxford Univ. Press, 1975.

Jahn, Janheinz. *Muntu: An Outline of the New African Culture*. Trans. Marjorie Grene. New York: Grove, 1961.

Johnson, James Weldon. *Autobiography of an Ex-Colored Man*, in *Three Negro Classics*. New York: Avon, 1968.

Jones, Gayl. *Corregidora*. New York: Random, 1974.

———. *Eva's Man*. New York: Random, 1976.

Kelley, William Melvin. *A Different Drummer*. New York: Doubleday, 1962.

Killam, G. D. "Language and Theme in *Things Fall Apart*." *Review of English Literature* 4 (Oct. 1964): 39–43.

Konadu, Asare. *A Woman in Her Prime*. London: Heinemann, 1967.

Lamming, George. *In the Castle of My Skin*. New York: Collier, 1975.

———. *Natives of My Person*. London: Michael Joseph, 1972.

———. *Of Age and Innocence*. London: Michael Joseph, 1958.

Larson, Charles. *The Emergence of African Fiction*. New York: Macmillan, 1972.

Laye, Camara. *The Radiance of the King*. London: William Collins, 1956.

Lévi-Strauss, Claude. *The Savage Mind*. Chicago: Univ. of Chicago Press, 1967.

Marshall, Paule. *Brown Girl, Brownstones*. New York: Avon, 1970.

Marx, Leo. *The Machine in the Garden: Technology and the Pastoral Ideal in America*. New York: Oxford Univ. Press, 1964.

Mbiti, J. S. *African Religions and Philosophy*. New York: Doubleday, 1970.

McKay, Claude. *Banana Bottom*. New York: Harper, 1933.

———. *Banjo*. New York: Harper, 1929.

———. *Home to Harlem*. New York: Harper, 1928.

Morrison, Alan P. "African Music," in *Continuity and Change in African Culture*. Ed. Melville Herskovits and William R. Bascom. Chicago: Univ. of Chicago Press, 1962.

Morrison, Toni. *The Bluest Eye*. New York: Pocket Books, 1972.

———. " 'Intimate Things in Place'—A Conversation with Toni Morrison," in *The Third Woman: Minority Women Writers of the United States*. Ed. Dexter Fisher. Boston: Houghton-Mifflin, 1980.

———. *Song of Solomon*. New York: Signet, 1977.

———. *Sula*. New York: Bantam, 1975.

Obiechina, Emmanuel. *An African Popular Literature: A Study of Onitsha Market Literature*. Cambridge: Cambridge Univ. Press, 1973.

Olney, James. *Tell Me Africa*. Princeton: Princeton Univ. Press, 1973.

Palmer, Eustace. *An Introduction to the African Novel*. New York: Africana, 1972.

Patterson, Orlando. *The Children of Sisyphus*. London: New Authors, 1964.

Raboteau, Albert J. *Slave Religion: The "Invisible Institution" in the Antebellum South*. New York: Oxford Univ. Press, 1978.

Ramchand, Kenneth. *The West Indian Novel and Its Background*. New York: Barnes and Noble, 1970.

Ravenscroft, Arthur. *Chinua Achebe*. London: Longmans, Green, 1969.

Rawick, George P. *From Sundown to Sunup: The Making of the Black Community*. Westport, Conn.: Greenwood, 1972.

Reid. V. S. *New Day*. New York: Alfred A. Knopf, 1949.

Roscoe, Adrian. *Mother is Gold: A Study in West African Literature*. Cambridge, England: Cambridge Univ. Press, 1971.

Schuyler, J. B., S. J. "Conceptions of Christianity in the Context of Tropical Africa: Nigerian reactions to its advent." In *Christianity in Tropical Africa*. Ed. C. C. Baëta. London: Oxford Univ. Press, 1968.

Soyinka, Wole. *The Interpreters*. London: André Deutsch, 1965.

———. *Season of Anomy*. London: Rex Collings, 1973.

Stevens, Wallace. "The Noble Rider and the Sound of Words." *The Necessary Angel*. New York: Random, 1958.

Tomsich, John. *The Genteel Endeavor: American Culture and Politics in the Gilded Age*. Stanford: Stanford Univ. Press, 1971.

Toomer, Jean. *Cane*. New York: Harper, 1969.

Turner, Darwin T. Introduction to Jean Toomer, *Cane*. New York: Liveright, 1975.

Updike, John. "Books: Shades of Black." *The New Yorker*, 21 January 1974.

———. *The Coup*. New York: Knopf, 1978.

Walker, Alice. *Meridian*. New York: Pocket Books, 1977.

———. *The Third Life of Grange Copeland*. New York: Harcourt, 1970.

Wästberg, Per. Introduction, *The Writer in Modern Africa: African-Scandinavian Writers Conference, Stockholm, 1967*. Uppsala: The Scandinavian Institute of African Studies, 1968.

Wellek, René and Austin Warren. *Theory of Literature*. New York: Harcourt, 1956.

Williams, John A. *Captain Blackman*. Garden City, N.Y.: Doubleday, 1972.

———. *Mothersill and the Foxes*. Garden City: Doubleday, 1975.

Wright, Richard. "Down by the Riverside," in *Ten Short Novels*. Ed. Thomas Ashton. Lexington, Mass.: Heath, 1978.

———. Introduction to George Lamming, *In the Castle of My Skin*. New York: Collier, 1975.

———. *Native Son*. New York: Harper and Row, 1940.

Index